アメリカ人が語る

日本人に隠しておけない

アメリカの"崩壊"

マックス・フォン・シュラー

AN AMERICAN SPEAKS

2ND CIVIL WAR：THE BATTLE FOR AMERICA

MAX VON SCHULER

ハート出版

Introduction
はじめに

In Japan, with the election of Donald Trump to the Presidency, people have noticed that there is something fundamentally amiss in the United States of America.

トランプ大統領の当選によって、ここ日本でも、「アメリカ国内では何かが根本的におかしくなっている」ということが分かってきました。

Where people are making the mistake is, they are believing American media claims that Donald Trump is absolute evil, and the cause of all of America's problems.

しかし、アメリカのマスメディアが声高に言う、トランプ大統領は最悪で、アメリカの全ての問題の原因であるというような主張をそのまま信じることは間違いです。

Not at all. The causes are much deeper, and have been building for a long time. Basically, the parties causing these problems are the American Corporate world and the American Left.

そうではなく、原因はもっと深く、長い時間をかけて進化してきました。基本的に、問題の原因は、アメリカの企業と左派なのです。

Education in America has been particularly taken over by Leftists in America. Now, with political correctness becoming one of the most popular causes in America, people are losing their jobs over saying a remark deemed to be unacceptable. There are cases of people being hounded into committing suicide.

特に、アメリカの教育は左派に乗っ取られています。ポリティカル・コレクトネスはアメリカで一般的な運動となり、ある人の発言が誰かを不快にさせたという理由で仕事まで失ってしまう可能性があるほど、社会に浸透しています。中には、その人が自殺に追い込まれるまで、いじめられたケースもあります。

Over a period of a few decades, virtually all college education has become dominated by radical Leftists.

ここまでの数十年間で、アメリカの大学教育は、ほとんどが急進的な左派に支配されてしまいました。

Political Correctness has become a philosophy of hate. It at first sounds like a good idea, promoting equality, but it's true goal is the destruction of present American society.

ポリティカル・コレクトネスは嫌悪（ヘイト）の哲学です。始めは、あたかも良い提案のように聞こえ、平等化を進める効果もありましたが、本当の目的は、アメリカの社会を崩壊させることです。

The Political Correctness movement in America has come to resemble the Cultural Revolution In Mao's Communist China.

アメリカにおけるポリティカル・コレクトネス運動は、かつての中国共産党が行った文化大革命に似ています。

Under the direction of Leftists, race relations, particularly between Black and White Americans, have deteriorated badly. Various universities now hold separate graduation ceremonies for Black students.

こうした左派による指導で、民族関係、特に白人と黒人の関係は、ひどく悪化しています。大学によっては、現在、黒人のみの卒業式を行っているところもあるくらいです。

はじめに

In this book, I describe what slavery was, a basic idea of how Black people have progressed, and the current trend of separatism for Black people which is pursued by the American left.

本書では、奴隷制度についても説明をし、それらが今までどのようにしてアメリカ社会における黒人の地位を向上させてきたのか、そして、現在の左派がそれをどのように利用して、黒人・白人の分離主義を遂行しているかを書いています。

This Civil Conflict is going to have great effect upon Japan. The ties between America and Japan are many and deep. In the last part of this book, I put forth some ideas of how Japan can cope when America is bedeviled by internal turmoil.

このアメリカの内戦は、日本にも大きな影響を与えます。アメリカと日本のつながりは深く、多岐にわたります。この本の終わりの方では、国内の混乱で悪魔に取りつかれたようになっているアメリカに対して、日本が対応するための方法、そして私からの提案を書いています。

It is time for Japan to prepare for a world where American power is much reduced.

日本は今こそ、今後やってくる、アメリカの影響力が非常に弱くなる世界に対する準備を始めるべきです。

Japanese people are hard working, intelligent, and highly innovative. I have faith in the Japanese people to be able to weather this storm.

日本人は一生懸命に働き、知識も豊かで、革新的な国民です。私は、日本人にはこの嵐を乗りきることができると、確信を持っています。

マックス・フォン・シュラー

Contents

Contents
もくじ

Introduction
はじめに／ 1

Chapter 1　2nd Civil War : The Battle for America
アメリカで二度目の内戦が始まる／ 10

The mass media's deceptive reporting
マスメディアによる偏向報道······························10

The wealth gap increases in America
アメリカ国内で広がる格差·····························15

The Deep State and the Globalists
ディープ・ステートとグローバリスト··················18

Chapter 2　The true roots of Political Correctness
ポリティカル・コレクトネスの本当のルーツ／ 21

The destructive poison of Political Correctness
国を破壊するポリティカル・コレクトネス··············21

Marxism and Political Correctness
マルクス主義とポリティカル・コレクトネス············25

Is America truly a free country?
アメリカは本当に自由の国なのか·····················29

Communist spies targeted military wives
軍人の妻を狙う共産党スパイたち·····················31

Interpreting the Declaration of Independence for your own benefit
独立宣言を都合よく解釈する人たち···················33

Feminists are mistaken about male/female equality
フェミニストたちの間違った男女平等··················36

The Left uses sexual minorities
左派に利用される性的マイノリティ･･････････････････38

The anti Vietnam war movement and the American Communist party
ベトナム反戦運動とアメリカ共産党･･････････････････43

Political Correctness running amuck
ポリティカル・コレクトネスの暴走･････････････････44

The "Cultural Appropriation" over reaction
「文化の盗用」に対する過剰な反応･･･････････････････47

Political Correctness and the problem of Black people
黒人問題とポリティカル・コレクトネス･････････････51

Some Black groups strongly protest the Civil War
南北戦争を否定する過激な黒人グループ･･･････････55

Americans are clueless about Japanese historical issues
日本の歴史問題に無関心なアメリカ人･･･････････････59

A staff member who complained about Clinton was killed
クリントンを告発して殺されたスタッフ･･･････････63

A people with no financial common sense
まともな金銭感覚を持たない人たち･････････････････65

A society full of hate
ヘイトが蔓延する危険な社会･･････････････････････67

The scary Feminist movement
恐るべきフェミニスト集団･･･････････････････････69

Why Americans tried to change Japan by provoking war
アメリカが日本を戦争に引きずり込んだ理由･･････････73

Chapter 3　America the ignorant
無知なアメリカ／76

The destruction of the American education system
崩壊するアメリカの教育システム･･････････････････76

Feminists alter history education
フェミニストによる歴史教育への介入･･･････････････79

The drugging of American students
クスリづけにされる子供たち･････････････････････83

Contents

Overly sensitive students
あまりにも敏感な学生……………………………………87

An education in self esteem
自尊心ばかりを持ち上げる教育…………………………90

Immature adults
大人だけど幼稚な人々……………………………………92

Selfish foreigners living in Japan
日本に暮らすワガママな外国人…………………………94

What is Christian Fundamentalism
キリスト教原理主義とは何か……………………………97

Chapter 4　The problem of race in America
アメリカの人種問題／ 100

Slavery in America and in the Roman Empire
アメリカの奴隷とローマ帝国の奴隷…………………100

Black people were brought forcibly to America
アメリカに「強制連行」されてきた黒人………………104

The separation of Black and White society
分断される白人社会と黒人社会………………………108

Integration succeeds in the military
軍隊では、人種の統合が成功した………………………113

Black people who are too sensitive to prejudice
差別に対して敏感すぎる黒人たち………………………115

The reality of a fragmented America
分断国家アメリカの現実…………………………………119

Chapter 5　Anti Trump and pro Trump forces
トランプ大統領に対する反対派と賛成派／ 122

Anti
反対派………………………………………………………122

The mass media do not report Black crime
メディアが報道しない黒人犯罪…………………………126

もくじ

The destruction of monuments from the Civil War
南北戦争に関する記念碑の破壊⋯⋯⋯⋯⋯⋯⋯⋯⋯⋯⋯129

Spoiled Black students
甘やかされる黒人学生たち⋯⋯⋯⋯⋯⋯⋯⋯⋯⋯⋯⋯⋯134

The structure of the Deep State
ディープ・ステートの正体⋯⋯⋯⋯⋯⋯⋯⋯⋯⋯⋯⋯⋯135

The meaning of supporting President Trump
トランプ大統領を支援する意味⋯⋯⋯⋯⋯⋯⋯⋯⋯⋯⋯138

The militia
民兵組織⋯⋯⋯⋯⋯⋯⋯⋯⋯⋯⋯⋯⋯⋯⋯⋯⋯⋯⋯⋯⋯142

Some notable militia actions
注目に値する民兵組織の活動⋯⋯⋯⋯⋯⋯⋯⋯⋯⋯⋯⋯145

Christian Fundamentalism
キリスト教原理主義⋯⋯⋯⋯⋯⋯⋯⋯⋯⋯⋯⋯⋯⋯⋯⋯148

President Trump and the Christian Right
トランプ大統領とキリスト教右派⋯⋯⋯⋯⋯⋯⋯⋯⋯⋯152

The United States Armed forces
アメリカ軍⋯⋯⋯⋯⋯⋯⋯⋯⋯⋯⋯⋯⋯⋯⋯⋯⋯⋯⋯⋯155

Political Correctness and the American military
アメリカ軍とポリティカル・コレクトネス⋯⋯⋯⋯⋯159

The continuing blunders of the US military
失態が続くアメリカ軍⋯⋯⋯⋯⋯⋯⋯⋯⋯⋯⋯⋯⋯⋯⋯163

The acute incompetence of the US military
アメリカ軍の深刻な無能化⋯⋯⋯⋯⋯⋯⋯⋯⋯⋯⋯⋯⋯165

The weakened American military that Leftists want
左派が目指すアメリカ軍の弱体化⋯⋯⋯⋯⋯⋯⋯⋯⋯⋯169

Chapter 6　Where America is headed, and what Japan should do
アメリカの今後と日本の進むべき道／ 171

The unavoidable collision between Right and Left
避けられない右派と左派の衝突⋯⋯⋯⋯⋯⋯⋯⋯⋯⋯⋯171

American education tilts to the Left
ますます左傾化する教育現場⋯⋯⋯⋯⋯⋯⋯⋯⋯⋯⋯⋯175

Contents

The movement to demonize the Right
右派を悪者にしようとする動き……………………179

The runaway out of control Left
コントロールを失い暴走する左派………………181

The prospect of terror attacks by the Left
左派によるテロ攻撃の可能性……………………185

Who can craft a solution?
誰が事態を収束させるのか………………………188

The Left can't see reality
左派には真実が見えていない……………………191

What should Japan do?
日本の進むべき道…………………………………193

A flood of American refugees
押し寄せるアメリカからの難民…………………196

How can American refugees live in Japan
アメリカ難民と日本人の共存……………………200

The LGBT issue in Japan
日本におけるＬＧＢＴの問題……………………203

Economic policy after the American collapse
アメリカ崩壊後の経済政策………………………205

TPP was not about Free Trade
ＴＰＰは自由な貿易ではない……………………207

Chapter 7　The problems of Defense after the collapse of America
アメリカ崩壊後の防衛問題／ 210

The crucial need to expand the Self Defense Forces
自衛隊の増強が不可欠……………………………210

Article No.9 does not protect Japan
憲法９条は日本を守ってくれない………………214

Do not be deceived by enemy propaganda
敵のプロパガンダにだまされるな………………216

The Emperor is central to a peaceful and prosperous Japan
天皇陛下を中心とする、豊かで平和な日本……221

もくじ

The miscalculations of the Deep State
黒幕たちの誤算……………………………………………223

Chapter 8　The Great Escape
大脱走／ 228

The extravagant escape plans of the Rich
富裕層の華麗なる逃亡計画…………………………228
Japanese people should learn from history
日本人は、今こそ歴史に学ぶべき………………………230

Afterward
おわりに／ 232

Sources
情報源／ 236

Chapter 1
2nd Civil War : The Battle for America
アメリカで二度目の内戦が始まる

The mass media's deceptive reporting
マスメディアによる偏向報道

Merchants have no country. The mere spot they stand on does not constitute so strong an attachment as that from which they draw their gains. —— Thomas Jefferson

商人に国境はない。彼らにとっては、国よりも利益が大切なのだ。
——トーマス・ジェファーソン(第3代アメリカ合衆国大統領)

They call him Donald Trump. Just that. That is how you can read the mass media referring to the President of the United States. It is extremely rude. For example, I did not particularly like former President George Bush the son, but I always referred to him as the President.

Thomas Jefferson
(3rd President of the United States)

トーマス・ジェファーソン
(第3代アメリカ合衆国大統領)

第1章　アメリカで二度目の内戦が始まる

　アメリカのマスメディアによって書かれた記事を読むと、米国のトランプ大統領は、単に「ドナルド・トランプ」と呼び捨てにされています。これは、とても失礼なことです。例えば、私はジョージ・ブッシュ大統領（息子）のことが、あまり好きではありませんでしたが、それでも私は、常に彼のことを「ブッシュ大統領」と呼びました。

George W. Bush
(43th President of the United States)
ジョージ・W・ブッシュ
（第43代アメリカ合衆国大統領）

　That is common respect. Well, America today has fallen into a place where respect no longer matters. People around the world wonder how Americans could have elected Donald Trump as President. Well for one, the media have portrayed him as a complete idiot.

　これは、ごく一般的な尊敬の念です。まあ、現在のアメリカでは、常識的な尊敬などというものは、とっくにすたれてしまっていますが……。今、世界中の人々が、トランプ大統領の当選について不思議に思っているのではないでしょうか。まず、マスメディアは彼のことを、まるで愚か者であるかのように扱っています。

　He is not. But there is a reason for this. Basically, the major media in America are no longer independent news organizations. They merely spout the information that their corporate sponsors wish to have broadcast or printed. So we can think of American media as propaganda outlets.

　しかし彼は愚か者ではありません。ただ、このように表現される

には理由があります。まず、基本的にアメリカのマスメディアは、もう独立した報道機関ではありません。スポンサー企業がテレビで放送したい情報、新聞に印刷したい情報しか出しません。もはや、アメリカのマスメディアは、一種のプロパガンダ機関と考えた方がいいでしょう。

Donald Trump
(45th President of the United States)
ドナルド・トランプ
（第 45 代アメリカ合衆国大統領）

Remember how CNN was constantly reporting how Hillary Clinton was leading in the 2016 election? The Huffington Post, a pro Feminism news source, was particularly bad in the respect.

2016 年の大統領選の時、CNN は常に、ヒラリー・クリントン氏がリードしていると報道していたのを覚えていますか？　ハフィントン・ポストやフェミニスト系のニュース媒体は、特にひどいものでした。

Hillary Clinton
(67th United States Secretary of State)
ヒラリー・クリントン元国務長官

第1章　アメリカで二度目の内戦が始まる

They were not reporting news, but what their corporate sponsors wanted to be true. From what I saw, of the major news organizations only Reuters and Rasmussen were accurate.

彼らはニュースを配信しているのではなく、自分たちのスポンサー企業の「希望」を配信していました。私が見る限り、大手ニュース機関では、ロイターとラスムッセン・レポートだけが正確でした。

So why did President Trump win? Americans can no longer live. The average American can no longer hope for an improvement in his living situation.

それではなぜ、トランプ大統領は当選することができたのでしょう？　今や、一般的なアメリカ人は、自分たちの国で暮らしていくことができていません。彼らは、その生活状況の改善を望むことすらできない状態なのです。

Normal society, social structures people used to believe in are failing. An appendicitis operation can cost $90,000. 700,000 Americans go bankrupt from Health care cost each year.

普通の社会、人が今まで信じてきた社会の構造というものが、だんだんと破壊されてきています。今、アメリカにおいて盲腸の手術を受けると、約900万円の費用がかかると言われています。毎年70万人ものアメリカ人が、医療の問題で自己破産しているのです。

Outsourcing has devastated the American Middle class. And tricky government accounting figures disguise the real number of unemployed people.

工場などを海外へ移転する、アウトソーシングの流れは、アメリカの中流階級を崩壊させてしまいました。政府は、狡猾な会計方法で、失業者の本当の数を隠しています。

13

Chapter1 2nd Civil War : The Battle for America

It is the American working class who voted for Donald Trump to become President. For them, he is hope.

そうした中、大統領選挙でアメリカの労働者階級の人々が、ドナルド・トランプ氏に投票をしました。彼らにとって、トランプ氏は希望なのです。

And this is despite a completely negative media campaign against him. Yes, the American mass media did not report, they conducted an anti Trump pro Clinton cheering campaign.

トランプ氏は、マスメディアのひどく否定的なキャンペーンにも関わらず、大統領になりました。ご存じのように、アメリカのマスメディアは、すでに報道ではなく、反トランプ、クリントンびいきの戦術をとりました。

President Trump takes the oath of office at the Inauguration Ceremony

大統領就任の宣誓をするトランプ氏

This is easy to prove. If they had truly done research, reporting, they would have found that support for Donald Trump to become President was strong in most of rural America. Instead, they provided cheering for the political figures their corporate sponsors liked. That was Clinton.

このことは簡単に証明できます。公平にリサーチをしたら、ほとんどのアメリカの地方で、「トランプ氏を大統領に」いう支持の声が強いことが分かったでしょう。しかし、マスメディアはその代わりに、「スポンサー企業の好きな」政治家を支持しました。それが、クリントン氏でした。

America used to have such great giant figures in the news media as Walter Cronkite, or Edward Murrow. Now it seems that American journalists simply read scripts written by some one else.

アメリカには以前、ウォルター・クロンカイト氏、あるいはエドワード・R・マロー氏のような、素晴らしいジャーナリストがいました。しかし、現在のジャーナリストたちは、ただ他人が書いた台本を読んでいるだけのように見えます。

The wealth gap increases in America
アメリカ国内で広がる格差

An American young person who graduates from university in America has so much debt that they cannot make a life.

現在、アメリカの大学を卒業する若者は、あまりにも負債が多すぎて、苦しい生活を送っています。

And the primary reason for this is corporate greed. When I first arrived in Japan, I was amazed that almost everyone was middle class, there were

Chapter1 2nd Civil War : The Battle for America

few really poor people. And it took me few years to really grasp how the Japanese employment system worked. I was very surprised to find out that people are rarely fired.

　その根本的な理由は、欲張りな企業の貪欲さです。私が初めて日本に来た時、ほとんどの日本人が中流クラスで、極端に貧乏な人は少ないということに驚きました。日本の正社員システムを理解するまでには数年かかりましたが、まず、働いている人がめったにクビにならないことに非常に驚きました。

In America it happens all the time.

　一方、アメリカでは、クビはよくあることです。

The Japanese National Health Insurance program is a marvel. I can personally say that it has probably saved my life when I had to go the hospital. And my family did not go bankrupt to support me.

　日本の国民健康保険のシステムも、とても素晴らしいものです。私自身も、このシステムのおかげで命を救われました。もちろん、私の家族は自己破産などしていません。

Another great thing about Japanese companies is that they will take an inexperienced person and train them. In America, this doesn't happen. American firms think of a person as a part in a machine. They put it in, and discard it when no longer needed.

　日本企業のもう一つの素晴らしいところは、経験がない人を訓練するということです。アメリカでは、このようなことをしません。アメリカの会社では、従業員を機械の一つの部品として考えています。ですから、必要な時に雇い、必要がなくなれば切り捨てます。

Japanese companies would take a person in, train him, and keep him. Yes, there were long hours, and people worked hard. But they were part

第1章 アメリカで二度目の内戦が始まる

of group, and treated importantly as such.

しかし日本の会社は、人を雇い、訓練して、その先もずっと雇用します。まあ、勤務時間は長いですが、それでも人々は一生懸命に働きました。社員はみんな、会社の一員として、会社から大切に扱われました。

Unfortunately, more and more Japanese employers are turning to American styles of management, and we can see the results of such things as the Akiba incident of 2008, were 7 people were killed. The murderer could not adjust to such a temporary lifestyle were at every work place he was treated as a part in a machine instead of as a human.

ですが、残念ながら、だんだん日本の会社が、アメリカの経営スタイルになってきています。そうしたことの一つの結果として、2008年に秋葉原の通り魔事件で7人が殺されました。その犯人は、どの職場でも、人間としてではなく、機械の一部として扱われ、そうしたことに適応することができなかったと言われています。

One reason this system worked for so long in America always had a frontier to the West. Disaffected people could leave and try their luck there. Well, about 120 years ago, that frontier disappeared. There no longer is anywhere to go.

この、アメリカ式のシステムが長い間アメリカで成功していた一つの理由は、西部の辺境があったからです。システムに不満を抱える人は西へ行き、未開拓の地域で頑張ります。まあ、120年前くらいに、そのような未開拓の地域はなくなってしまい、現在は、逃げられる場所もありませんが。

In the present day, we call these selfish predatory capitalists Globalists. They are driven by extreme greed. In 1983, the average pay of a CEO in Fortune 500 companies was 38 times that of the average worker. Now it is

17

Chapter1 2nd Civil War : The Battle for America

224 times.

昨今では、このような利己的で略奪的な資本主義者を、「グローバリスト」と呼びます。彼らはますます、その貪欲さによって駆り立てられています。1983 年にフォーチュン誌が発表した、主要500 社の代表取締役の平均的なギャラは、普通の労働者の 38 倍でした。それが、現在では 224 倍です。

This wealth gap has drawn media attention. But while media pundits discuss what it means, it has transformed America and the world.

こうした格差は、マスメディアの注目をひきました。しかし、評論家たちが、この格差の意味を討論している間にも、格差はアメリカと世界の国々に、どんどん広がっていきました。

The Deep State and the Globalists
ディープ・ステートとグローバリスト

There is also the Deep State. These are behind the scenes people, some military, some corporate, some in government, who rule America for their own goals and profit.

そこには、「ディープ・ステート (Deep State)」という存在もあります。日本語では、「政治的な黒幕」とでも言えばよいでしょうか。このような人たちは、企業、官僚、軍人、政治家の中にいて、自分たちの利益のためにアメリカを支配しています。

Together, the Globalists and the Deep State have created a revolutionary situation in America.

こうしたディープ・ステートとグローバリストは、アメリカに革命のような状態を作り出しました。

第1章　アメリカで二度目の内戦が始まる

And that is why, despite the efforts of Globalists and the Deep State, Trump won the Republican nomination, and then the election.

そしてそれは、ディープ・ステートとグローバリストの画策を押しのけて、トランプ氏が共和党の指名を獲得し、大統領選挙に勝利した理由でもあるのです。

The people who supported Donald Trump for President can be called traditionalists, and supporters of the Constitution of the United States.

大統領選でドナルド・トランプ氏を支持した人たちは、伝統主義者、そしてアメリカ合衆国憲法を守る人たちと呼ぶことができます。

Japan has a central pillar of society in the Imperial household, and is very lucky for that. America does not have a Monarchy, but does have a Constitution. It is the traditionalists who regard this as the central pillar of the United States.

日本では皇室が社会の中心の柱となっており、それはとても素晴らしいことです。一方、アメリカには君主制はありませんが、憲法があります。伝統主義者は、この憲法を、アメリカの中心の柱と考えています。

There is also a Marxist Left wing in the United States, that seeks to create Marxist revolution. During the Vietnam war, they were quite open with street riots against that war.

もちろん、アメリカにもマルクス主義の左派はいます。彼らの目標は、アメリカでマルクス主義の革命を起こすことです。ベトナム戦争の時には、反戦暴動を行いました。

They also bear some of the responsibility for The Great Pacific War between Japan and America. Marxists inside the Franklin Roosevelt administration played a large role in encouraging President Roosevelt to

19

Chapter1 2nd Civil War : The Battle for America

pressure Japan until Japan attacked Pearl Harbor.

　彼らマルクス主義者には、日本とアメリカの間で戦われた大東亜戦争への責任もあります。なぜなら、フランクリン・ルーズベルト政権の中にいたマルクス主義者たちには、ルーズベルト大統領を日本が真珠湾攻撃を行うまで扇動するという、大きな役割がありました。

Violent clashes have increased between these two sides, until we can say that America stands on the verge of Civil War.

　現在、アメリカ国内では右派と左派の暴力的な衝突が増えており、アメリカは間もなく、内乱（Civil War）になると言われています。

Let's take a look at these two sides.

　本書では、二つの側面を中心に見ていきたいと思います。

The Anti-Trump forces.

　反トランプ派、

Feminists and Political Correctness.

　そして、フェミニストとポリティカル・コレクトネスの問題です。

20

Chapter 2
The true roots of Political Correctness
ポリティカル・コレクトネスの本当のルーツ

The destructive poison of Political Correctness
国を破壊するポリティカル・コレクトネス

America is beginning to dissolve into chaos. There was nearly a week of riots after the election. In late January 2017, President Trump calls for a temporary ban on immigrants for certain Muslim nations.

アメリカが大混乱に陥り始めています。まず、大統領選挙後に、1週間くらいの暴動がありました。2017年1月末に、トランプ大統領がいくつかのイスラム教国から、一時的に入国を禁止すると提案したためです。

He wishes to review screening procedures to keep out terrorists.

トランプ大統領は、テロリストがアメリカに入国できないように、その調査手続の見直しをしようと考えています。

This has happened before. In 2011 President Obama suspended immigration from Iraq for six months after two guerrillas who had killed Americans with bombs in Iraq were found in Kentucky.

ただ以前にも、同じようなことがありました。2011年に、オバマ大統領がイラクからの移民受け入れを、半年間、中止したのです。それは、イラク戦争においてアメリカ兵を爆弾で殺したゲリラが、アメリカ国内のケンタッキー州で見つかったためでした。

Chapter2 The true roots of Political Correctness

It happened several times before that, notably just before WWII when President Franklin Roosevelt placed restrictions on European Jews to enter the US. He feared that Nazi spies would sneak in.

アメリカの歴史では、フランクリン・ルーズベルト大統領が数回、このような入国禁止令を行い、特に第二次世界大戦の前には、ヨーロッパのユダヤ人に対して入国制限を行いました。こうしたユダヤ難民の中にナチスのスパイが隠れ、アメリカに入国してくる恐れがあったためです。

The American Left made massive, well organized protests at airports across the nation.

トランプ大統領の入国禁止令に対してアメリカの左派は、組織的で大規模な抗議を、全国の空港で行いました。

President Trump signs the immigration ban order
入国禁止の大統領令にサインをするトランプ氏

第 2 章　ポリティカル・コレクトネスの本当のルーツ

But watching Japanese television, people are saying President Trump's first two weeks are chaos.

一方、日本のテレビを見ていると、評論家たちが、「トランプ大統領の最初の 2 週間が、混乱の中で始まった」と言っています。

They say America is a free country, his temporary ban on Muslim people from some countries is awful.

また彼らは、「アメリカは自由の国なのに、このトランプ大統領の一時的なイスラムに対する入国禁止令は、ひどいことである」と言っています。

These people, including some Americans, do not understand America.

しかし、この評論家たち、ある種のアメリカ人も含めて、どれもアメリカを理解していません。

First of all, President Trump's temporary ban is seen as very popular by many Americans. Right wing Americans are very tired of traditional Washington politics. When President Trump came up with the phrase "Drain the Swamp" when referring to the capitol in Washington, it resonated with many people.

まず、トランプ大統領の一時的な入国禁止令は、数多くのアメリカ人の共感を集めています。右派のアメリカ人は、伝統的な「ワシントン政治」というものに、うんざりしているのです。トランプ大統領が、ワシントンの州議事堂に対して "Drain the Swamp"（沼の水を排出、この場合は、悪者を追い出すこと）と言ったことに、数多くのアメリカ人が喜びました。

Americans on the Right will feel this is decisive action. Over the last few decades, political correctness promoting diversity has grown into a religion.

23

Chapter2 The true roots of Political Correctness

右派のアメリカ人にとって、これは決定的な動きです。最近の数十年間、多様性を進めるポリティカル・コレクトネスは、宗教のようになってしまいました。

And if people are from a minority group, they are given preference in employment and other areas. Yes, the truth is that America has always been a land of prejudice. I know. My mother's parents immigrated from Sweden, and it was hard.

マイノリティ（少数派）は、雇用やその他のことで、常に優先されています。本当は、アメリカは昔から差別の国なのです。私は、それをよく知っています。私の母の両親はスウェーデンから移民してきたので、大変でした。

The problem with the concept of diversity is that it actually creates disunity. America is a land of many different people. But they must all speak the English language. They must all behave by certain laws. We cannot go by culture here, because all the cultures of the world are so different.

多様性の概念に関する問題点は、実は、それが不和を生み出すということにあります。アメリカは、様々な人種でできている国です。しかし、全員が英語をしゃべる必要があり、特定の法律に従う必要があります。アメリカでは、文化を基準にしていたら生活ができません。なぜなら、様々な人種による世界の文化は、あまりにも違いすぎるからです。

Political Correctness, by emphasizing differences, and enforcing them, is actually creating disunity and is destructive to the nation.

ポリティカル・コレクトネスは、文化の違いを強調し、それを人々に強要することで、実は不調和を作り出し、国を崩壊させているのです。

第2章　ポリティカル・コレクトネスの本当のルーツ

This is being disguised as protecting people's rights. Actually, diversity is not about helping minorities, it is about forcibly changing the life of the majority of people. It is about the destruction of present society, and it is a Marxist philosophy.

これは、あたかも人々の権利を守ることであるかのように偽装されています。しかし真実は、こうした多様性は少数派を助けるためのものではなく、大多数の人を強制的に変えることで、現在の社会を崩壊させるという意味なのです。これはマルクス主義の哲学です。

Marxism and Political Correctness
マルクス主義とポリティカル・コレクトネス

Let us look at a little history. It my writings, I have written that political correctness began in the 1960's with protests against the Vietnam war. Well, to be more exact, that is when it began to become prominent in American society.

ここでちょっと、歴史を振り返ってみましょう。私は、ポリティカル・コレクトネスの始まりは、1960年代の反ベトナム戦争の抗議活動だと考えています。これは厳密には、その時に、ポリティカル・コレクトネスがアメリカの社会で目立つようになり始めた、ということです。

It actually began in the 1920's, with a group of Marxist Philosophers who founded the Frankfurt School in Germany. Their goal was to destroy Western civilization, and create a perfect Marxist society. They were very dismayed by the failure of the European working class to revolt after the horror of the First World War.

ポリティカル・コレクトネスの本当の始まりは、1920年代にド

25

Chapter2 The true roots of Political Correctness

イツのマルクス主義の哲学者グループが、フランクフルト学派を創設したことです。彼らの目標は、西洋文明を崩壊させることで、この世界に完璧なマルクス主義の社会を作り上げることでした。しかし、第一次世界大戦という惨事の後で、革命どころではないヨーロッパの労働者たちは、狼狽しました。

So they began to look for a different kind of Marxism. Instead of fomenting revolution based on the economy and class, they began to think of making revolution based on culture.

そこで彼らは、違う種類のマルクス主義の実現を探し始めました。経済と階級に基づいて扇動するタイプの革命ではなく、文化に基づいた革命というものについて考え始めたのです。

As a matter of interest, Richard Sorge, who became a Soviet spy in Japan during WWII, was a member of this group.

ちなみに、大東亜戦争の時に日本で暗躍したソ連のスパイ、リヒャルト・ゾルゲ氏は、このグループの一人でした。

One of their members, Erich Fromm, came up with the idea that masculine and feminine roles were determined by society and are oppressive.

そうしたメンバーの一人、エーリヒ・フロム氏が、「男性と女性の役割は社会によって決められており、これは抑圧的である」という考え方を提唱しました。

Their main philosophy was called "Critical Theory". This means unrelenting criticism of Western society.

彼らの主要な考え方は「批判理論」と呼ばれていました。これは、西洋社会への容赦ない批判を意味します。

第2章　ポリティカル・コレクトネスの本当のルーツ

We can see this concept in work today on the political American Left. There is a website for children called "Queer kid stuff". It encourages homosexuality and transgenderism among children. It teaches things like, when a child is born, a doctor "assigns" the child sex based on physical genitals. But this is not the child's " true" sex. That is what the child themselves feel.

現在のアメリカ左派の活動にも、この哲学を見ることができます。ネット上に "Queer kid stuff" というウェブサイトがあります。ここでは、子供たちにゲイ（同性愛）やトランスジェンダー（性転換）を奨励しています。例えば普通、赤ちゃんの性別というのは、お医者さんが赤ちゃんの性器を見て「割り当てて」いるものですが、これは子供の本当の性別ではなく、本当の性別はその子供の気持ちで、自分で決めるものである、というのです。このようなことを、このサイトでは子供たちに教えています。

Well, this is some very dangerous thinking. Children are often naturally confused about sexual roles. They often do not solidify until after puberty. Adults should not interfere with the process in any way. A few will turn out to be Gay, but the overwhelming majority of children will be heterosexual. This is natural.

これは、とても危険な考え方です。子供たちは混乱して、自分の性別というものが、よく分からなくなってしまいます。たいていの場合、彼らの思春期が終わるまで、よく分からないままになるでしょう。大人がこういうことに関して邪魔をしてはいけません。確かに一部の人たちはゲイになるかもしれませんが、ほとんどの子供は異性愛者になります。これは自然なことです。

But the politically correct movement is encouraging children to think of themselves as something different sexually from how they were born. And children will try to please adults, who try to influence them that they are gay or trans. A child should be let alone to work out such things when

27

Chapter2 The true roots of Political Correctness

they become adult.

　しかし、ポリティカル・コレクトネスの運動家たちは、子供たちに対して、生まれた時の性別とは違う性別になることを奨励しています。子供というのは、大人を喜ばせたいものです。なので、そうした大人が子供にゲイとかトランスジェンダーを積極的に教えることは、とても危険なのです。そういうことは、子供が大人になってから、自分で決めるべきです。

The Frankfurt school saw encouraging sexual ambiguity as a way to destroy Western society. We should also notice here that they really had no idea what sort of society should arise in it's place.

　トランスジェンダーを推し進める人々にとって、性別の曖昧さは、

The Twitter account of "Queer kid stuff" (https://twitter.com/queerkidstuff)
「Queer kid stuff」のツイッター・アカウント

第2章　ポリティカル・コレクトネスの本当のルーツ

西洋社会を破壊する道でした。しかし、実際にどのような新しい社会を作りたいのかということは、曖昧なままでした。

Is America truly a free country?
アメリカは本当に自由の国なのか

When Adolf Hitler came to power in Germany, these Marxist philosophers fled Germany to America, where they were sponsored by Columbia University.

ドイツでアドルフ・ヒトラーが支配者になった時、このマルクス主義の哲学者たちはアメリカへ逃げました。その彼らを支援したのが、コロンビア大学でした。

Most of them returned to Germany after the war. However one man who stayed in America, Herbert Marcuse, was to play a pivotal role in the America Left wing movement.

戦後、彼らは、ほとんどがドイツへ帰りました。しかし、アメリカに残った一人、ヘルベルト・マルクーゼ氏が、アメリカの左派運動の中心的な役割を担うことになりました。

It was the Frankfurt school people who came up with concept of victim groups such as Gays, Blacks, and women.

こうしたフランクフルト学派は、「犠牲者」のグループ、例えば、黒人、ゲイ、女性といった「社会的弱者」の概念を考え出しました。

Japanese people think of America as a free country. No, not really. There are many rules, and for most of history, it was a rather strict society. If you were not White, Anglo Saxon and Protestant, you were a second or

29

Chapter2 The true roots of Political Correctness

third class person.

　たいていの日本人は、アメリカは自由の国であると思っていますが、実はそうでもないのです。ルールがたくさんあり、アメリカは、そのほとんどの時代において、かなり厳格な社会でした。アングロサクソン系の白人でなければ、二流か三流の国民という扱いでした。

For example, Gays used to hunted.　In rural areas they were actually killed.　That still happens today.　In the cities, Gay bars would be raided. The names of Gay people arrested would be published in the newspaper. This would destroy the lives of some people.

　例えば、かつてゲイの人は、「狩り」の対象でした。現在でも時々ありますが、田舎では実際にゲイたちが殺され、大都市ではゲイバーに警察の手入れがありました。逮捕されたゲイの人たちの実名が新聞に載せられ、数多くの人たちが、こうした行為により人生を壊されました。

So America has never been a really free country.　When I was in the Marine Corps, I have written that I was an undercover Naval Intelligence agent.　I worked inside an American Communist party spy cell outside my base in Iwakuni Japan in 1975.

　そう、アメリカは昔から、全く自由の国などではありません。以前の本にも書きましたが、私はアメリカ海兵隊の時代に、海軍情報部局の秘密調査員でした。そして、1975年には、山口県岩国市の米軍基地の外で、アメリカ共産党員のスパイ集団の中に入り込んで活動をしていました。

However, one of my superiors was an avid Gay hunter.　At that time, it was illegal to be in the military if you were Gay.　If such a person was found, they would be given a less than honorable discharge.

　私の上司の一人は、熱心な「ゲイ・ハンター」でした。当時、ゲ

30

第2章　ポリティカル・コレクトネスの本当のルーツ

イの入隊は違法でしたので、そのような人が見つかると、軍隊から不名誉な形で除隊させられました。

In 1969, at a Gay bar called The Stonewall in New York City, the patrons fought back against a police raid. This was the true beginning of the Gay Rights movement in the US.

1969年、ニューヨーク市ストーンウォールのゲイバーで、ゲイの客たちが警察の手入れに反撃しました。これが、アメリカでのゲイの権利運動の始まりでした。

As everybody knows, Black people have had a difficult and terrible history in America. I will devote a chapter to them later.

また、誰もが知っているように、黒人の人々はアメリカにおいて、とても困難で、恐ろしい歴史を持っていますが、それについては、のちほど詳しく取り上げたいと思っています。

Communist spies targeted military wives
軍人の妻を狙う共産党スパイたち

White American women are very spoiled and pampered. Yes, it is true that until the women's liberation movement started men were often condescending to them, but we can not say that as a group they suffered as much as racial minorities. They are very jealous of the attention given to Black people as a class since the Civil Right moment of the 1960's.

アメリカの白人女性は、とても大切に扱われ、甘やかされています。まあ、女性解放運動（ウーマン・リブ）が始まるまでは、男性は女性に対して恩着せがましい態度をとっていましたが、それでも、白人女性たちが少数民族のように苦しめられるということはありま

31

Chapter2 The true roots of Political Correctness

せんでした。むしろ、1960年代の公民権運動で黒人たちが注目されるようになると、白人女性はそれに対するヤキモチを焼き、そうした黒人たちを、ねたむようになりました。

So there actually was, and still is, a lot of prejudice and injustice in American society. This gave the Marxist philosophers of the Frankfurt school great opportunity.

過去から現在に至るまで、アメリカ社会には、大量の差別と不正義が存在します。これは、フランクフルト学派のマルクス主義哲学者にとって、非常に大きなチャンスでした。

Herbert Marcuse became the father of the politically correct movement in the US. I particularly remember American Communist Party spies in Japan discussing his theory of "polymorphous perverse" while I was a Naval Intelligence agent. This was a theory promoting sexual activity outside the norms of what society could accept. The American Communists also recruited a few wives of Marines into their movement.

アメリカでは、ヘルベルト・マルクーゼ氏は、ポリティカル・コレクトネス運動の「父」となりました。私は特に、海軍情報部の秘密調査員をしていたころ、日本におけるアメリカの共産党スパイたちが「多形倒錯」という彼の論文について話をしていたのを覚えています。この論文では、社会で一般的に許容される範囲を超えた性的行動を奨励しています。アメリカの共産党スパイたちは、何人かの海兵隊の奥さんたちをスカウトしていました。

The truth is, being the wife of a military member can be difficult. The military member is often deployed for extended periods of time, meaning he is sometimes sent across the planet. For a wife left back in a base in Japan, it can be very harsh.

実際のところ、軍人の奥さんたちの生活は大変です。軍人は長期

にわたって派遣される場合があり、場合によっては、地球の反対側まで派遣されることさえあります。これは、日本の米軍基地に残っている奥さんたちにとっては、非常につらいことです。

The other military wives do try to help. But the Communists started on a few of these people with feministic type of propaganda, originally developed by Frankfurt school philosophers.

他の軍人の奥さんたちも、何かと手助けをします。しかし、そうした隙間に共産党のスパイが入り込み、フランクフルト学派の哲学者が開発したフェミニズムのプロパガンダを利用して、奥さんたちをスパイとしてスカウトしたのです。

However, in the time I was in Iwakuni, the Communists never had any great intelligence successes.

それでも、私が岩国基地にいたころは、こうしたアメリカの共産党スパイたちも、大した成果はあげられていませんでした。

Interpreting the Declaration of Independence for your own benefit
独立宣言を都合よく解釈する人たち

In the protests that are occurring across the nation now against President Trump, they have all the hallmarks of Communist activity.

現在のアメリカで行われているトランプ大統領への抗議は、実は共産党の活動であるという証拠があります。

The American Left who espouses political correctness on American university campuses is not interested in discussion. They shout down any person who expresses another kind of idea. University professors who say

Chapter2 The true roots of Political Correctness

something not deemed politically correct are fired. It is the students who decide this. A professor who said in class that the primary job of women is to raise children was fired.

現在、アメリカの大学でポリティカル・コレクトネスを奨励している アメリカの左派たちは、討論というものに興味がありません。 自分と異なる意見を言う人には、大声をあげて黙らせます。もし大 学の先生がポリティカル・コレクトネスに合わないことを言えば、 その先生はクビになります。しかもそれを、学生たちが決めるので す。例えば、ある大学の先生は、「女性にとってメインの仕事は、 子供を育てることだ」と言って、クビになりました。

University administrators have abdicated their authority, given up to the students.

大学の当局者たちは、彼らの権限を放棄し、それを学生たちに明 け渡してしまいました。

This has become excessively terrible. The post election protests, the protests against President Trump's decision to temporarily halt immigration from some Moslem countries are both organized and classically Communist.

こうした状況は、どんどん酷くなっています。トランプ大統領に 対する選挙後の抗議、トランプ大統領の出したイスラム教国からの 入国禁止令に反対するための抗議は、伝統的な共産主義者のやり方 で、組織的に行われているのです。

When President Obama did it in 2011 the American Left did nothing.

2011 年、オバマ大統領が同じ入国禁止令を行った時には、アメ リカの左派は何もしませんでした。

The Left is saying that they fight for human Rights. Well this sounds

第 2 章　ポリティカル・コレクトネスの本当のルーツ

very good. But what do Human Rights truly mean? In America, we have the phrase "The Right to the pursuit of Happiness". It is in the American Declaration of Independence. But look closely at the sentence. The word "pursuit" is very important.

　こうした左派は、自分たちは人権のために戦っていると言います。まあ、この言葉だけを聞けば、何か良いことのように聞こえるでしょう。しかし、人権とは本来、どのような意味ですか？　アメリカには「幸福追求の権利」というフレーズがあります。これは、アメリカの独立宣言に書いてあります。しかし、この文章をよく見てください。この、「追求」という単語はとても大切です。

It means to chase after something. But it does not guarantee it. What this phrase in the Declaration of Independence means is that because of your birth, your race, economic class or any other factor, no one can stop your attempt to achieve happiness, or satisfaction, or success.

　追求とは、何かを追い求めるという意味です。しかしそれは、保証されるという意味ではありません。独立宣言のこの言葉が意味するものは、人の生まれや民族、経済的な豊かさによって、その人の、幸福、満足、成功するための試みを、誰かが止めること、邪魔をすることはできない、ということなのです。

But nowhere does it guarantee you success, or happiness. Only that you may attempt it. This is what so many Americans do not understand. They believe that they have a right to satisfaction no matter what.

　つまり、幸福や成功は、なんら約束されていないのです。ただ、それを試みることができる、ということだけが約束されているのです。しかし多くのアメリカ人は、このことを理解していません。彼らは、なにがなんでも満足する権利がある、と信じています。

The present day American Left is using this concept to destroy

Chapter2 The true roots of Political Correctness

traditional America. They will take a racial or sexual minority, and make extreme demands upon other people for that minority. But these demands are designed to irritate or to destroy the lives of others.

現代のアメリカの左派は、アメリカという国を壊すために、この発想を利用しています。民族であったり、性的な少数派であったり、そうした人たちを選んでは、その少数派のために極端な要求をします。こうした要求は、その他の人たちを怒らせ、あるいは彼らの人生を奪うように、計画的に考えられています。

When the majority balk at satisfying such extreme demands, the Left screams "prejudice"!

大多数の人たちがこの極端な要求に難色を示した場合には、左派が「差別だ！」と叫びます。

Feminists are mistaken about male/female equality
フェミニストたちの間違った男女平等

Feminists are exactly the same. They say they want equality for the sexes. It sounds like a good thing at first. But the sexes are not equal. Physical strength is quite different. The way men and women think is quite different.

フェミニストたちも、完全に同じです。彼らは、口では男女平等を求めていると言います。これも、始めは良いことのように聞こえますね。しかし、男女は決して同じではありません。肉体的な特徴が違います。また、考え方も違います。

The point here is not to think of one sex as different than the other, or superior to the other, but that they complement each other to make a family. American Feminists try to make men and women the same, but it cannot work. And American Feminists always think in terms of which sex

36

第2章　ポリティカル・コレクトネスの本当のルーツ

is more powerful, or superior to the other.

　ここで大切なのは、男女がどう違っているか、あるいは、どちら
が優れているかと考えることではなく、お互いに補いあって家族を
作り上げていく、ということです。アメリカのフェミニストたちは、
男性と女性を同じ状態にしたいようですが、それは無理です。彼ら
フェミニストは、いつも、どちらがより強いのか、あるいは優れて
いるのかという視点で考えています。

Their actions are designed to destroy what they perceive as male
superiority, and to create and enforce female superiority. This emphasis on
conflict between male and female is why they have never really succeeded
with their philosophy in Japan.

　フェミニストの活動は、男性優位とされているものを破壊し、女
性優位を作り出し、それを相手に強要することです。この、男女の
対立を強調する考え方は、アメリカ発のフェミニズムが日本で成功
していないことの、大きな理由でもあります。

Women are not suited for combat roles in the military. They are
physically weaker, and sexual attraction between men and women is
disastrous in a military situation. The Israeli army gave it up after the
1973 Yom Kippur war. Combat units with women in them tended not to
fight but to surrender easily.

　女性は、軍隊での戦闘任務には適していません。肉体的に男性よ
り弱いし、男女間の性的な魅力は、前線で戦闘を行っている部隊で
は特に、面倒な問題を引き起こすでしょう。第四次中東戦争におけ
る1973年のヨム・キプルの戦い以降、イスラエル軍は、女性兵士
に前線で戦闘する任務を与えることをやめました。なぜか。女性が
所属する前線部隊は、すぐに戦うことをあきらめ、簡単に降伏して
しまうからだそうです。

37

Chapter2 The true roots of Political Correctness

In general, women are much better at emotional decisions than men. We should not try to force each sex to be the same as the other, but to understand each other.

基本的に、感情的なものごとを決定する時には、男性よりも女性の方が優れています。強制的に男女を同じものにしようとするのではなく、お互いを理解しようとすることが大切です。

The Left uses sexual minorities
左派に利用される性的マイノリティ

Personally, I am not concerned with unusual sexual behavior. In Japan, people might have what to other people looks like an average marriage. But secretly, they may engage in all sorts of different sexual activity. Well, that is fine.

個人的に私は、他人の「普通じゃない」性生活については気にしません。日本では、普通の結婚生活を送っているように見える夫婦が、ひそかに、いろいろと普通じゃない性行為をしているということがあるのかもしれませんが、まあ、それはそれで良いでしょう。

However Western societies have a Christian base. And, according to most versions of Christianity, sexual activity is closely regulated. This is often extended into law governing sexual behavior. Basically, any kind of sex outside of a marriage between a man and a woman, was regarded as crime for much of America's history.

一方、西洋の社会には、キリスト教という基盤があります。ほとんどのキリスト教の宗派で、性行為は厳しく管理されています。この、性行為を管理するということは、その社会の法律となることもあります。アメリカの歴史において、たいていの場合、男女の結婚

第2章　ポリティカル・コレクトネスの本当のルーツ

以外の性行為は犯罪でした。

What is Trans Genderism? It is a person who feels themselves to be the sex opposite of what they physically are. They are about 0.03% of the population. Well, the truth is there is a tremendous variety of sexual practices and minorities in the world.

トランスジェンダーとは何でしょう？　それは、自分の肉体的な性別とは逆の、心の性別を持っているということです。おおよそ、人口の0.03%の人は、トランスジェンダーだと言われています。実際、世の中には数多くの性行為のパターンがあり、少数派もたくさんいます。

But sexual activity should be a private affair between the people involved. As long as no one is physically injured, and as long as children are not involved, I do not think it is a problem.

しかし性行為は、当事者にとっては、きわめてプライベートなことです。ケガをしたり、子供を巻き込んだりしない限り、それは問題にはならないでしょう。

What is happening in America is the Left is trying to force their concepts upon all of America. I have lived in New York City. It is not uncommon to see a man dressed openly as a woman walking the in the street. Well, in New York City, nobody would really care about that.

現在のアメリカが抱える問題は、左派が自分たちの考えを強制的にアメリカ全土に押し付けようとしていることです。私はニューヨーク市に住んだことがありますが、街なかで女装している男性を見ることは、めずらしくありませんでした。まあ、ニューヨークでは、誰も他人のやることを気にしませんが。

But in Nebraska, which is a very conservative rural state, it would be the

39

Chapter2 The true roots of Political Correctness

cause of trouble. People there do not like people who openly push such difference.

しかし、これが例えば保守的な田舎の州であるネブラスカ州では、トラブルの原因になります。そこに住む人々は、そのような目立つ人を嫌います。

A recent and ongoing problem in America with Trans gender people is public toilets. Trans gender people are demanding the right to use public toilets of their choice in any area of the United States. They say that if this right is not granted to them, it is discrimination.

現在のアメリカで、大きなトランスジェンダーの問題となっているのは、公衆トイレの問題です。トランスジェンダーの人たちは、アメリカ合衆国のどこであろうと、自分が選んだ性別に合う公衆トイレを利用する権利を主張しています。この権利が与えられなければ、それは差別であると言っています。

Well, in a literal interpretation, that is true. However, let us look at the problem from an idea of common sense. If the Trans gender people had limited their demands to say, New York City or San Francisco, where there are many such people, there never would have been a political problem in the United States.

表面的な解釈をすれば、それは正しいのかもしれません。しかし、常識的な面からこの問題を考えてみましょう。もし、こうしたトランスジェンダーの人たちが、その要求をニューヨーク市とかサンフランシスコ市のような、トランスジェンダーとゲイの人が多いところを限定して行っていたら、アメリカでも政治的な問題にはなっていないでしょう。

But to try to force Nebraska to do this is only going to create resentment and trouble. In any case, Gay, Trans gender people, if they are born in

40

第2章　ポリティカル・コレクトネスの本当のルーツ

such rural areas, tend to migrate to more liberal big cities.

　しかし、ネブラスカ州でこのようなことを強制しようとすれば、そこには怒りやトラブルしか生まれません。だから結果的に、たとえトランスジェンダーやゲイの人がそのような地方で生まれたとしても、ほとんどの場合、彼らは大都市へと移住してしまうのです。

So there would be very few such people in Nebraska. But by forcing such laws on rural areas, and the Obama administration did put much pressure on them, the American Left is creating violent confrontations.

　だからネブラスカ州では、トランスジェンダーやゲイの人が少ないのです。しかし、オバマ政権がこのような法律を地方にも強制するために、かなりの圧力をかけました。このようにして、アメリカの左派が、国内に暴力的な争いの場を作り出しているのです。

This is their goal. They are using such sexual minorities to help start a Left wing revolution. To maintain a society, there has to be common sense. To satisfy the desires of one person, it is not right to harm the desires of thousands.

　これは左派の目的です。性的マイノリティを利用して、左翼革命を実現しようとたくらんでいるのです。こうした勢力から社会を守るためには、常識が必要です。一人の欲求を満足させるために、何千人もの人々が損害をこうむることは、決して正しいことではありません。

Another thing. In Japan, unusual types of sexual activity are not at all a problem. But America has a basically strict Christian background. Basically, any kind of sex outside of marriage is proscribed, and especially homosexuality.

　もう一つは、同性愛のことです。日本では、法律の範囲内で行われる様々な性行為は、特に問題になりません。しかしアメリカでは、

41

Chapter2 The true roots of Political Correctness

基本的に厳しいキリスト教が、社会の基礎となっています。基本的に、結婚外のどんな性行為も禁止であり、特に同性愛は禁止です。

In Japan, this is not a problem. Japan is a much more free country than America.

日本では、このことは問題になりません。日本はアメリカより自由な国です。

And when Americans say America is free, what do they mean? What they mean is political freedom. You have the right to call the President an idiot. But there has never really been social freedom in America.

それでは、アメリカ人が「アメリカは自由な国である」と言う時、それはどのようなことを意味するのでしょうか？ まず、アメリカでは政治的な自由があります。自国の大統領をバカと呼ぶ権利があります。しかしアメリカも、始めから社会的な自由があったわけではありません。

America has many legal laws that are strictly enforced. For example, public drunkenness is a crime. You can be arrested for walking drunk. Not in Japan! And if what you say offends someone, you can be attacked socially for being politically incorrect, and perhaps lose your job.

アメリカは、厳しい法律によって守られています。例えば、公共の場での泥酔は犯罪です。酔っ払って街を歩いていたら逮捕されます。でも、日本では違います！ それと、もしあなたの話すことで、誰かが失礼だと感じた場合、ポリティカル・コレクトネスに反するという理由で、社会的な攻撃を受ける可能性があり、それによって仕事まで失うかもしれません。

For a person coming from a third world country that is extremely impoverished, or in the middle of Civil War, America could be a free country.

第2章　ポリティカル・コレクトネスの本当のルーツ

　非常に貧しい国とか、内戦が続く国から来た人にとっては、確かにアメリカは自由な国でしょう。

But for a person coming from Japan or Europe it is quite restrictive.

　しかし、日本人やヨーロッパの人たちにとっては、非常に制限が多い国です。

The anti Vietnam war movement and the American Communist party
ベトナム反戦運動とアメリカ共産党

However in America now we have a prime example of a revolutionary situation.　There have not been such massive protests since the anti Vietnam war movement of the 1960's.

　率直に言って、現在のアメリカは革命の状態にあります。1960年代の反ベトナム戦争運動からこのかた、このように大規模な抗議行動はありませんでした。

Having been a Naval Intelligence agent, who worked with Communist anti war Americans at the end of the Vietnam war, it is my estimate that some 5% to 10% of Americans involved with the anti-war movement were actual Communists.

　私は、ベトナム戦争の終わりに、米海軍情報部局の秘密調査員として、アメリカ共産党のグループに潜入しましたが、私の見積もりでは、反ベトナム戦争運動のメンバーの5%から10%は、共産主義者だったと思われます。

The rest were simply average American young people who did not want to fight in Vietnam.

43

Chapter2 The true roots of Political Correctness

その他は、単純にベトナムで戦いたくないという、一般的なアメ
リカの若者でした。

But the lives of average Americans in 1975 were the most prosperous in
American history. Average Americans were not going to make a violent
Communist revolution. Even the lives of Black people were improving,
they were moving into the middle class.

しかし、1975 年の当時、一般的なアメリカ人の生活はアメリカ
の歴史上、最も豊かでした。そうした一般的なアメリカ人は、暴力
的な共産主義革命を望みません。しかも、黒人たちの生活も徐々に
よくなってきて、彼らもだんだんと中流階級に加わっていきました。

After the Vietnam war ended, people lost interest in protest. The
Communists retreating into Academia, on American university campuses,
and the Feminist movement took on a Communistic tone. Gradually over
time, non Leftist professors were purged from universities, and Feminists
became more and more radical.

ベトナム戦争が終わると、アメリカの人々は抗議することに対す
る興味を失いました。そこで、共産主義者たちは、活動の場所を学
界、つまりアメリカの大学へと移しました。フェミニズムの運動も、
だんだんと共産主義化していきました。少しずつ、左派ではない教
授がパージ（排除）されていき、フェミニズムはますます過激にな
りました。

Political Correctness running amuck
ポリティカル・コレクトネスの暴走

By the time of the 2016 Presidential election, university campuses had
become centers of politically correct tyranny. Any small thing, a simple

word spoken, could lead to a professor being fired. Commentators outside the university correctly called this a Maoist crusade.

2016年の大統領選挙まで、アメリカの大学ではポリティカル・コレクトネスの暴政が席巻し、どんな小さなこと、たった一つの発言でも、教授がクビになりました。大学外の評論家たちは、このような行為を「毛沢東主義的な粛清」と呼んでいます。

Even the English language is being completely reworked. For example, the words "He" and "She" are considered to be sexually discriminatory. The word "Ze" is to take their place.

英語という言語すら、作り直そうとされています。例えば、英語の "He"（彼）と "She"（彼女）は、現在では性的な差別用語であると考えられています。そして、これからの性別として、中立的な "Ze" を使うことを勧めています。

In America, if you own a business, it is too dangerous to put up a sign saying "Merry Christmas" in December. You are likely to be sued by someone who says you are prejudiced against non Christians.

もしあなたがアメリカでビジネスを行っている場合、12月に「メリー・クリスマス」という看板を出すことは危険です。誰かに、「あなたは、キリスト教の信者ではない人を差別している！」と裁判で訴訟を起こされることになるでしょう。

If you get married in California, you cannot use the words "Man and Wife" or "Husband and Wife" in the ceremony. You must use something gender neutral like "Spouse and spouse". Otherwise it is felt that you might offend gay people.

もしあなたがカリフォルニア州で結婚式を挙げる場合、式の最中に「夫と妻」という言葉を使うことは、法律的に不可能です。これからは性的に中立な言葉、「配偶者と配偶者」を使わなければなり

45

Chapter2 The true roots of Political Correctness

ません。なぜなら「夫と妻」という言葉は、ゲイの結婚に対して失礼であるからです。

Every Halloween, there is much screaming and yelling about some celebrity who wore a Halloween costume deemed offensive. In 2016, a singer/actress named Hillary Duff dressed as a pilgrim, her boyfriend, Jason Walsh, dressed as an Indian, and they appeared at a Halloween party.

ハロウィーンの仮装をめぐっても、いつも多くの争いごとが起こります。ある時、あるセレブのハロウィーン・コスチュームが不適切であると判断されました。2016年に女優で歌手のヒラリー・ダフさんが、ピルグリム（アメリカに渡った清教徒）のコスチュームを着て、そして彼女のボーイフレンドはアメリカ・インディアンのコスチュームを着て、パーティーに参加したのです。

They were very harshly criticized in the media for being politically incorrect. There is no social freedom in America.

彼らは、ポリティカル・コレクトネスを守っていないという理由で、マスメディアから厳しく批判されました。このように、アメリカでは、社会的な自由はないのです。

A friend asked me about earrings. It seems that Latino students at Pitzer College in Claremont California object to White girls wearing large hoop earrings. They said that such earrings are symbols of oppression and exclusion for non White students.

ある時、ある友達からイヤリングについて質問されました。カリフォルニア州クレアモント市のピッツァー大学で、白人女性が大きな輪っか状のイヤリングを耳につけていることに対し、ラテン系の学生が反対しているというのです。そのラテン系の学生の主張は、そのようなイヤリングは有色人種の学生に対する抑圧と排除の象徴であるということです。

46

第 2 章　ポリティカル・コレクトネスの本当のルーツ

Students at Oberlin college in Ohio objected to Sushi and Vietnamese food being served in the school cafeteria. Students said the rice was under cooked, and the food was not made with cultural sensitivity.

オハイオ州のオーバリン大学では何人かの学生が、食堂で出している寿司とベトナム料理に反対していました。その学生たちの主張では、お米が正しく調理されておらず、文化的な配慮をもってその料理が作られていないことが問題だということです。

So perhaps next they will demand that Japanese restaurants in America stop serving the California roll, and other rolls like the Boston roll? These Sushi rolls are made in America creations. And while they are not accurate to the original in Japan, when I lived in New York City and worked in Japanese restaurants, I found such creations to be interesting and delicious.

そうなると次は、アメリカの日本料理店がカリフォルニア巻きやボストン巻きを提供することを禁止する要求をするのではないでしょうか？　なぜなら、この巻き寿司は、アメリカで創作された「日本系」アメリカ料理だからです。確かに日本の巻き寿司と同じではありませんが、私はニューヨーク市に住んでいたころ、面白い、美味しい食べものだと思いました。

Under political correctness, such innovation and creativity would be forbidden.

つまり、ポリティカル・コレクトネスによって、このような革新、創造性は、すべて禁止になるのです。

The "Cultural Appropriation" over reaction
「文化の盗用」に対する過剰な反応

The use of cultural aspects considered unique by one culture, by people

47

Chapter2 The true roots of Political Correctness

of another culture is called "Cultural Appropriation".

　ある文化におけるユニークな面を、別の文化を持つ人たちが利用すると、すぐさま「文化の盗用だ」と言われてしまいます。

Some Japanese readers might say that such comments are childish, and university students need to mature and grow up.

　日本の読者の皆さんは、このようなコメントに対して、子供っぽい、その学生たちは大人になるべきだ、と思われるかもしれません。

Well I agree that that is very true, but these actions have real consequences in American life, outside the college campus.

　まあ、それはその通りで、私も同意しますが、こうした彼らの動きは、大学の外にあるアメリカ人たちの生活にも、影響を与えるのです。

Justin Bieber received a lot of criticism for wearing dreadlocks. Dreadlocks are considered unique to Black people. I have seen a video of a Black woman student attacking a White male student for wearing dreadlocks. She told him angrily that he should not do that.

　例えば、歌手のジャスティン・ビーバー氏がヘアスタイルをドレッドヘア（縮れた髪を細かく編んだヘアスタイル）にした時に、たくさんの批判を受けました。アメリカでは、ドレッドヘアは黒人特有のものと考えられているからです。私は、ある動画をネットで見たことがあります。大学の中で、白人の男子学生がドレッドヘアをしているからという理由で、黒人の女子学生が彼を殴っているビデオです。彼女は激怒して、「そのようなヘアスタイルをするべきではない！」と叫んでいました。

In February of 2017 Vogue magazine ran a photo shoot of a White female model, Karlie Kloss, wearing Japanese kimono.

第２章　ポリティカル・コレクトネスの本当のルーツ

2017 年 2 月、ファッション雑誌ヴォーグが、白人女性のモデル、カーリー・クロスさんが日本の着物を着た写真を誌面に出しました。

There were fierce protests against the magazine, that it is improper for White people to wear a Japanese kimono.

これに対し、ヴォーグ誌には、強い抗議が寄せられました。なぜか。ポリティカル・コレクトネスでは、白人が日本人の着物を着ることは不適切だからです。

In the summer of 2015, The Boston museum of fine arts had to cancel an interactive exhibit. The painter Claude Monet made a painting of his wife wearing a Japanese kimono, titled "La Japonaise". In the Boston museum interactive exhibit, people could wear a kimono of the same pattern in front of the painting and have their picture taken.

2015 年夏には、ボストン美術館がインタラクティブ（双方向性）を取り入れた展示会を中止しました。画家のクロード・モネは、彼の妻が日本の着物を着ている作品「ラ・ジャポネーゼ」を描きましたが、ボストン美術館では、参加者が絵と同じ模様の着物を着て、絵の前に立って写真を撮るという、インタラクティブな展示が企画されました。

Protesters, three of them demonstrated outside the museum, demanding that the museum cease the exhibit as it was racist cultural appropriation.

すると 3 人の抗議者が美術館に対してデモを行い、この展示は人種差別的な文化の盗用であるから展示をやめるようにという要求をしました。

The reason that the museum cancelled the exhibit in the face of only three protestors is fear. In modern America, there is very much a conformist mindset among the people who espouse politically correctness. If the museum did not back down, those three protesters would have

49

Chapter2 The true roots of Political Correctness

been joined by many. Articles would have appeared in newspapers and magazines on how racist the museum was. It very well could have been on the television news.

　ボストン美術館がたった３人の抗議者で展示を中止した理由は、「恐れ」です。現代のアメリカでポリティカル・コレクトネスを支持している人たちは、実に協力的です。もしボストン美術館が展示をやめない場合、その３人の抗議者は、あっという間にたくさんの抗議者に増え、新聞と雑誌に、「ボストン美術館は非常に人種差別的である」という記事が書かれます。さらに、テレビのニュースにも取り上げられたかもしれません。

The director of the museum would have been forced to step down. The actual question of whether indeed the exhibit was racist does not matter. What matters is the social sense of the people protesting.

　このボストン美術館の館長は、強制的にクビにされました。その展示が本当に人種差別的だったかどうかは関係ありません。大切なのは、「抗議者の社会的な気持ち」なのです。

Modern America is now ruled by such an atmosphere of fear, many people are afraid of speaking because they may be labeled politically incorrect.

　現在のアメリカには、このような恐怖の雰囲気が、どこでもあります。ほとんどの人は、「ポリティカル・コレクトネスがない！」と言われることを恐れ、めったに自分の意見を言いません。

And this is a large reason for the popularity and victory of President Trump. He speaks out and says what he thinks. Half of America is tired of the tyranny of political correctness.

　そしてこれは、トランプ大統領が当選した大きな理由でもあるのです。彼は、自分の考えていることをはっきりと言います。つまり

50

第 2 章　ポリティカル・コレクトネスの本当のルーツ

アメリカ人の半分は、ポリティカル・コレクトネスの横暴さに、うんざりしているのです。

Political Correctness and the problem of Black people
黒人問題とポリティカル・コレクトネス

Political Correctness in America has run amuck.

アメリカでは、こうしたポリティカル・コレクトネスが荒れ狂っています。

There were, and still are, many words in American English that are very insulting, that deny your humanity. For example the word "Nigger". It is so sensitive that Americans cannot say it, even to say it is bad. When Americans refer to this word, they say the "N" word, or write it like this: "N_____".

昔から英語には、とても失礼な、人間性を否定する言葉が数多くあります。例えば、"Nigger"（ニガー／黒人を指す蔑称）です。この言葉は敏感すぎて、たいていのアメリカ人は使えません。もし、どうしてもこの単語が使いたい場合は、「N の単語」と言います。文字に書く時には、「N_____」のような書き方をします。

But of course many people still use it in an insulting fashion to Black people. And to confuse things, Black people use it among themselves.

それでもまだ、数多くの人が、黒人に対してこの言葉を侮辱的に使っています。ただ不思議なことに、時々は黒人どうしで使っていたりもします。

But my advice to my readers: If you travel in America, never ever use

51

Chapter2 The true roots of Political Correctness

this word. It will only lead to serious trouble.

ここで、読者の皆さんへ私から忠告です。もしあなたがアメリカを旅するなら、絶対に、この単語を使ってはいけません。きっと、大きく深刻なトラブルを引き起こすでしょう。

So political correctness evolved to eliminate such insulting words from the American English language. At first it seemed like a good idea.

そもそもは、このような侮辱的な単語を英語から浄化するためにポリティカル・コレクトネスが進化しました。だから、始めのうちは、多くの人が良いことだと思ったのでしょう。

But in reality it became a lot like Newspeak in George Orwell's novel 1984. People want to create a perfect world, are extremely sensitive.

しかし、現実的には、ジョージ・オーウェル氏の小説『1984』のニュースピーク（作中の全体主義国家が作った新しい英語）のようになっています。こうした、非常に敏感なアメリカ人たちは、パーフェクト・ワールド、つまり完全な世界を作りたいのです。

With American education, the emphasis is on not exposing people to things that they don't like. Safe spaces are provided so that people can avoid things that trouble them.

アメリカの教育では、学生の嫌がることには触れないようにする、ということを重視しています。学校内に、学生たちが自分の嫌いなものを避けて隠れることができる、安全な場所が提供されています。

For example, recently New York schools attempted to ban words from use in school like dinosaur, because it would offend children who did not believe in evolution, divorce, because it would offend children whose parents divorced, and birthday, because Jehovah's Witness religious doctrine does not celebrate birthdays.

第 2 章　ポリティカル・コレクトネスの本当のルーツ

　ニューヨーク市の学校で、最近このような提案がありました。それは、いろいろな単語を学校で使用禁止にする、というものでした。例えば、「恐竜」は進化論を信じない子供に失礼、「離婚」は自分の親が離婚した子供に失礼、「誕生日」はエホバの証人の信者に失礼(エホバの証人の教義では、誕生日を祝うことは禁止です)。

But what this produces is people who are physically adult but emotionally and spiritually children. And they are extremely arrogant emotional children, in a country that possesses enough nuclear weapons to destroy the planet.

　しかし、このような教育システムは、肉体的には大人でも、精神的・感情的には子供、という人間を作ります。とても傲慢で感情的な、子供のような大人。しかも彼らの国は、地球をすべて破壊し、人類を絶滅させるのに十分な数の核兵器を持っているのです。

Political correctness has also evolved to excuse poor performance by minorities. For example, you cannot correct a Black person's English in American schools. This is regarded as prejudiced, since the Black person came from poor schools, or that some people think that speaking a broken dialect of English is Black culture.

　学校では、マイノリティの人たちの成績が悪い時の言いわけに利用するために、ポリティカル・コレクトネスが進化しています。例えば、アメリカの学校で、黒人の英語の間違いを指摘することは禁止です。彼らの間違いを指摘して直すことは「差別」だと考えられています。なぜか。これは、その黒人が劣った学校から進級してきた、という偏見になるから。あるいは、その英語の(間違った)表現は、黒人独自の文化であると考慮されるからです。

And this kind of attention does not really help minorities. In the 1960's era of civil rights demonstrations, Black people wanted equality with all Americans.

53

Chapter2 The true roots of Political Correctness

でも、このような扱いは、本当の意味でマイノリティを助けることにはなりません。そもそも 1960 年代の人権デモで、黒人たちは、黒人以外のアメリカ人との平等化を希望したではありませんか。

Now they demonstrate for separation, and enshrinement of victim status. This is a classical Marxist type of philosophy. America can only be weakened by such actions.

現在、彼らは、他のアメリカ人とは別の生活をし、自分たちを犠牲者の状態にずっと置いておいてもらうためにデモをします。これは、古典的なマルクス主義の哲学です。このような活動によって、アメリカが弱められていくのです。

Americans come from many lands, many cultures. To maintain a nation, people must learn the English language. Ebonics is a Black American dialect of English. To get an idea of what is like listen to the lyrics of Rap music.

アメリカ人の先祖は、多くの国、多くの文化圏からやって来ました。このような国を維持するために、皆が英語を学ぶ必要があります。「エボニックス」は、黒人たちが作ったアメリカ英語の方言です。どのような方言であるか聞いてみたい場合は、黒人たちの歌うラップ・ミュージックを聞いてみてください。

But it is not a true language. In this modern day of excessive political correctness, there are many figures who are pushing for the education of Black people in Ebonics, saying that it is their "culture".

しかし、それは本当の言語ではありません。現在の過度なポリティカル・コレクトネスの時代では、多くの人が、アメリカ黒人を、このエボニックスで教育した方がいいと言っています。なぜなら、それが黒人の文化であるから、という理由です。

Well it may be that it is the culture of some Black Americans, but if they do not learn proper English, they will always be a separate inferior group in American society. Perhaps this is a goal of American Left wing Marxists.

まあ、それは確かにアメリカ黒人文化の一部かもしれませんが、正しい英語を学ばなければ、アメリカの社会では、永遠に下位のグループになります。おそらくは、それがアメリカの左派、マルクス主義者の目指す目標なのでしょう。

Some Black groups strongly protest the Civil War
南北戦争を否定する過激な黒人グループ

And America can no longer make decent movies. In the year 2015 there was an outcry nationwide over the Confederate battle flag in the American Civil War of 1861 to 1865. There were calls to ban the movie "Gone with the Wind" because it was felt that it might make people sympathetic to the Confederate cause.

アメリカはもはや、良い映画を作ることができません。2015年に、南北戦争（Civil War：1861 ～ 1865）の、連合国（南軍）の国旗に対して、アメリカ全土で大反発する抗議がありました。そして、南北戦争における南部の白人を描いた映画「風と共に去りぬ」を上映禁止にせよとの意見が多数ありました。なぜかというと、その映画を見ると、多くの人が南の連合国に対して共感するかもしれないから、というのです。

But the facts of the matter are that the North did not start that war to free the slaves. And that there were some freed Black soldiers in the Confederate Army.

Chapter2 The true roots of Political Correctness

しかし、北の連邦政府は、奴隷を自由にするために戦争を開始したわけではありませんでした。そして、南の連合政府軍には、自由な黒人兵士もいました。

Recently, the Confederate flag has been banned from Federal cemeteries and National parks, even if the soldiers who lie in those graves fought for the Confederacy.

近年では、この南部の国旗は、連邦政府の管理墓地と国立公園で掲げることが禁止されています。そのお墓の中の兵士が、南軍のために戦ったのだとしても、南部の国旗は禁止なのです。

This angers me very much, my ancestors fought on both sides. We should respect the dead.

私は、このことに対して、大きな怒りを感じます。我々は、国のために命を失った兵士を尊敬しなければなりません。

The truth is, Americans are still fighting the American Civil War of 150 years ago in their hearts. For the Northern, White Liberal class, any hint of pride by Southern people concerning the war must be destroyed. It cannot be tolerated.

実際のところ、アメリカ人の心の中では、いまだにその150年前の南北戦争を戦っているのです。北部のリベラルな白人たちは、南部の人がその戦争について誇りを持っていれば、それを叩き潰さなければなりませんし、決して彼らのその誇りを許しません。

But the war was not about slavery. At least at first. If President Lincoln had declared that he wished to fight to end slavery, the Northerners would not have fought.

しかも、その戦争は奴隷を解放させるためのものではありませんでした。少なくとも、戦争開始の時はそうでした。もしリンカーン

第 2 章　ポリティカル・コレクトネスの本当のルーツ

大統領が奴隷制度を終わらせるために戦争をすると宣言していたら、北部の人たちは戦わなかったでしょう。

So instead, emotional issues, that the South could not secede from the Union, could not be independent, were used. And then the North started an aggressive war upon the South. The South just wanted to be left alone.

だから、その代わりに感情的なこと、例えば、アメリカ南部の連邦政府からの脱退禁止が戦争開始の理由であると説明されました。それによって、北部側が攻撃的に南部側を侵略したのです。南部側の連合政府は、ただ自分たちの生活をしたかっただけなのです。

If I spoke to an American from the North, and said that I was proud of my Confederate ancestors, I would be verbally attacked.

今でも、もし北部で生まれたアメリカ人に対して私が、自分の南の連合国の先祖に誇りを持っていると言ったら、きっと私は相手から言葉による攻撃を受けるでしょう。

Such northern people would assume that I hate Black people, that in my heart I am some enemy of America. Of course, not at all.

そのような北部の人は、私のことを「黒人に嫌悪の気持ちを持っている、潜在的なアメリカの敵」だと考えるでしょう。もちろん、そうではありません。

Recently, in May of 2017, the city of New Orleans has begun to take down memorials to prominent Confederate generals and leaders of the Civil War. This effort has been spearheaded by a Marxist professor named Malcolm Suber. He leads the group Take 'em down NOLA.

2017 年 5 月からニューオーリンズ市は、南北戦争の有名な南の将軍やリーダーの記念碑を取り壊し始めました。この活動は、Take 'em down NOLA（ニューオーリンズで白人優位のすべての

57

Chapter2 The true roots of Political Correctness

シンボルを下ろす）という、マルクス主義の黒人教授、マルコム・スーバー氏がリーダーを務めるグループが行っています。

This group wants to rewrite the history of the American Civil War. And he has openly said that his next target will be statues of George Washington, because he also owned slaves.

このグループは、南北戦争の歴史を書き直すことを望んでいます。リーダーのマルコム・スーバー氏は、次の目標はジョージ・ワシントンの記念碑であると、はっきり言っています。なぜなら、彼も元は奴隷の雇い主でしたから。

These very radical Black are a minority, but under the rules of Political

The Twitter account of "Take 'em down NOLA"
(https://twitter.com/takeemdownnola)

「Take 'em down NOLA」のツイッター・アカウント

Correctness now in force in America, the destructiveness of these people cannot be discussed.

　このような過激な黒人は少数派ですが、今やアメリカでは、ポリティカル・コレクトネスのルールによって、この人たちの破壊性を議論することは不可能となっているのです。

And one must remember, 18% of Black Americans voted for President Trump.

　でもここで、一つの真実を覚えておきましょう。アメリカ黒人の18％が、トランプ大統領を支持し、彼に投票したということを。

Americans are clueless about Japanese historical issues
日本の歴史問題に無関心なアメリカ人

Traditional Communist tactics call for rewrites and revisions of history, and that is what these Marxists are doing here.

　伝統的な共産党の戦術というのは、歴史の修正と書き直しを要求することであり、アメリカのマルクス主義者も同様に、それを行っています。

Just like The Great East Asian War. Americans really did not want to fight Japan or Germany. So President Roosevelt provoked Japan into attacking. They knew Pearl Harbor would be attacked, so only old battleships were there. Then it became easy to get Americans to fight.

　日本の大東亜戦争と同じです。アメリカ国民は、ドイツ、あるいは日本と戦争をしたくありませんでした。だから、ルーズベルト大統領は日本から戦争を開始するように扇動したわけです。アメリカ政府は真珠湾が攻撃されることを知っていましたので、真珠湾には

Chapter2 The true roots of Political Correctness

古い戦艦しかありませんでした。真珠湾攻撃のあとで、アメリカ人の気持ちを戦争に向かわせることは簡単でした。

Very few Americans understand history truthfully.

本当の歴史を理解しているアメリカ人は少ないです。

Many Japanese people hope that I can explain the truth of the Great East Asian War to Americans. They wish that I tell Americans that Japan was not an evil nation.

多くの日本人は、私がそうしたアメリカ人に対して、大東亜戦争の真実を説明することを望んでいます。歴史をよく知らないアメリカ人に対して、日本は悪の国ではなかった、ということを説明することを希望しているのです。

It is impossible.

しかし、それは不可能です。

Americans always bring up The Comfort Women problem, Nanking, and they always say that Japan was brutal in Korea.

アメリカ人は、永遠に、南京事件、慰安婦問題、それと、日本は朝鮮併合で朝鮮の人たちに残酷なことをした、という話を持ち出します。

The truth is, the Comfort Women system was very well run, any abusive brokers, who were mainly Korean, were punished by the Japanese government.

でも真実は違います。日本の慰安婦システムは、うまく機能していました。慰安婦たちを虐待するようなブローカー（それはだいたいコリアンの人でしたが）は、日本政府から罰せられました。

第2章　ポリティカル・コレクトネスの本当のルーツ

What happened at Nanking was an exception. And the Japanese Imperial Army restored discipline after the event. Something like that did not happen again. Even today, American troops commit many crimes, but too often American military authorities ignore them and hide them.

　南京事件は例外的な出来事でした。しかも、日本帝国陸軍は、その事件の後に軍の規律を厳しくし、組織として修復されました。だから、その後はそのような事件は二度と起こりませんでした。現在でも、アメリカの兵士たちは事件を起こし、犯罪を犯します。しかし、アメリカの軍当局は、ほとんどの場合、それらの事件を隠してしまいます。

The war in China was both a conventional war and a guerrilla war. And both wars are brutal. And Americans in war are horrible to other Americans. Read about Sherman's march to the sea in the American Civil War. It was marked by rape, pillage, and killing of civilians.

　中国での戦争は、通常戦とゲリラ戦の両方でした。そのどちらも残酷なものです。そして、戦争中のアメリカ人は、他のアメリカ人に対して残酷です。アメリカの南北戦争における焦土作戦、「シャーマンの海への進軍」を読んでください。そこでは、レイプ、略奪、一般国民の殺害などが、大規模に行われました。

As far the annexation of Korea, it was in total contrast as to colonization as practiced by European powers. Japan developed Korea to be equal to Japan. This is a process I call "uplift".

　日本の朝鮮併合は、ヨーロッパ列強による植民地支配とは対照的なものでした。日本は、当時の朝鮮を、日本と同じレベルまで発展させました。私はこれを「向上」と呼んでいます。

But Americans, in particular present day politically correct Americans, are not interested in truth. They wish to accuse, to find some wrong doing

61

Chapter2 The true roots of Political Correctness

somewhere. Then they can say they are good people.

　しかし、現在のアメリカ人、特にポリティカル・コレクトなアメリカ人は、そうした真実には興味がありません。誰かを告発したい、どこかで行われている不正を見つけて非難したい、という気持ちばかりです。そうすることで、自分は良い人間であると自慢することができるからです。

On the internet in America, such people are called "SJW". It means Social Justice Warrior. It is not a compliment. However this activity is dangerous. With all this screaming about how the South was evil in the American Civil War, all they have done is open another fault line in American society.

　アメリカのネットでは、こういう人々は、「SJW」と呼ばれています。その意味は "Social Justice Warrior"(社会正義のために戦う戦士)ということです。これは賛辞ではありません。それどころか、こうした行為は危険です。例えば、彼らが南北戦争で南部の連合国

Sherman's march to the sea in the American Civil War
南北戦争における「シャーマンの海への進軍」の様子

62

第2章　ポリティカル・コレクトネスの本当のルーツ

がいかに邪悪であったかを叫ぶことで、アメリカの社会に亀裂を作り出すからです。

There are many fault lines in American society today, and they threaten to rip America apart in a new bloody Civil War.

現在のアメリカ社会には、こうした亀裂が数多くあります。そして、こうした亀裂が新しい残酷な内乱をアメリカ社会に引き起こすのです。

A staff member who complained about Clinton was killed
クリントンを告発して殺されたスタッフ

When Hillary Clinton was chosen to be the 2016 Democratic party candidate, and her victory was rigged, completely fraudulent, the Feminist movement closed ranks around her. Anyone who spoke any objections to her candidacy, or asked about her corruption, was shouted down by Feminists as anti-women, simply prejudiced.

ヒラリー・クリントン氏は、2016年の予備選挙で民主党の候補に選ばれました。その予備選挙は不正であり、完全にインチキでしたが、フェミニズム運動家たちが彼女を守りました。彼女の立候補を疑った人、クリントン家の腐敗について質問をした人はすべて、こうしたフェミニストたちから女性差別者として攻撃されました。

This is classic Marxist technique. And this big story that still goes on, about Russian hacking and interfering in the election is a complete lie. It was meant to distract people from the Democratic corruption.

これもまた、古典的なマルクス主義のやり方です。さらに、何度も繰り返されるハッキングで、ロシアがアメリカの選挙に干渉した

63

Chapter2 The true roots of Political Correctness

というのも、全部、嘘です。その理由は、民主党の腐敗から人々の気をそらすためです。

And the truth is, the Russians had no major part in influencing the election of Donald Trump to the Presidency. The Democratic party cheated massively in favor of Hillary Clinton, one of their staffers leaked that information to Wikileaks.

ドナルド・トランプ氏の大統領選勝利に対して、ロシアからの影響はありませんでした。反対に、民主党はクリントン氏のために大規模な不正をしていたので、民主党のスタッフが、匿名の内部告発サイト「ウィキリークス」に、その不正をリークしました。

Soon after, he was found shot to death.

その直後、彼は射殺されました。

第2章　ポリティカル・コレクトネスの本当のルーツ

A people with no financial common sense

まともな金銭感覚を持たない人たち

The American corporate world has created the revolutionary situation. By simple greed, by increasing the wealth gap to obscene levels, Americans are angry. They cannot live.

アメリカの企業は、国内に革命のような状態を作りました。ひたすら企業の強欲さによって貧富の格差が深刻なレベルになり、一般的なアメリカ人たちは、こうした事態に怒っています。彼らは、このままでは生活ができません。

Extreme medical costs, outsourcing, extreme student loans that ensure lifetime debt for college students. The average American can now only look forward to a dismal future.

べらぼうに高い医療費、工場を海外などへ移転するアウトソーシングによる就職難、べらぼうに高い利息の学生ローンといったものは、学生たちに一生、借金を返済する生活しか約束しません。このままでは、一般的なアメリカ人の未来は真っ暗です。

And the average American has not behaved very well either. Everyone has credit cards, they use them freely for frivolous reasons. But a credit card is debt. Americans are always too optimistic that their situation will improve economically to cover the debt. It is not possible.

しかし、こうした一般的なアメリカ人も、まともな金銭管理を行っていません。アメリカ人は、ほぼ全員がクレジットカードを持っていて、つまらないもののために、簡単にカードを使っています。しかし、クレジットカードは借金です。アメリカ人は、いつも、そのうち自分の経済状態が良くなり、負債も軽くなると、あまりにも楽

Chapter2 The true roots of Political Correctness

観的に信じています。しかし残念ながら、それは不可能です。

So the greed of American corporations has done grievous harm to the United States. President Trump is doing his best to take some decisive action in a very short time. The economic problems in America are serious, and have built up over about three decades. It will be impossible to change everything in a short time.

その上で、さらにアメリカの企業の強欲さが、アメリカ社会に重大な損害を与えているのです。トランプ大統領は迅速に、決定的な措置をとるための最善を尽くしています。しかし、アメリカの経済問題は深刻で、30 年以上にわたって徐々にできあがりました。短期間で、これらすべてを改善することは不可能です。

People in Japan might ask, how could America's corporate elite be so shortsighted, so stupid? Japanese people might say, "Does it not take great intelligence to become the CEO of a major US corporation?"

アメリカの企業エリートはそんなに先見の明がない、そんなに愚かな人たちなのですか？と、日本人は疑問に思うかもしれません。普通の日本人なら、巨大なアメリカ企業の CEO や取締役になるためには、相当に頭がよくないと無理だと考えるでしょう。

Well, yes, that is true. But what Japanese people do not realize about Americans is that they have no intellectual curiosity. Of course, to become the CEO of a major corporation takes a lot of hard work. But the average CEO would just not be interested in other country's culture, foreign languages, art, or history. And that includes American history. Americans in general are not interested anything they do not need for work, to make money.

それは確かにそうです。しかし、アメリカ人には知的好奇心というものがない、ということを、多くの日本人は知りません。もちろ

第 2 章　ポリティカル・コレクトネスの本当のルーツ

ん、大企業の取締役になるためには、一生懸命に働くことが必要です。でも、一般的に、アメリカ企業の取締役たちは、他国の歴史や文化、芸術、言語などに興味がありません。それは、アメリカの歴史も含めてです。仕事のため、お金を儲けるために必要な知識以外には興味がないのです。

So they really would not have any idea that their actions are creating a situation for violent revolution. I also do not think Hillary Clinton was aware of the Socialist Marxist aspect of the Feminist organizations, or perhaps she just did not care. She simply wanted power.

だから、彼らの行っている行為が暴力的な革命につながる状態を作っている、ということが分からないのです。同じように、ヒラリー・クリントン氏も、フェミニズム運動のマルクス主義的な側面に気づいていなかった、あるいは、気にしていなかったのでしょう。彼女はただ、権力が欲しかったのだと思います。

A society full of hate
ヘイトが蔓延する危険な社会

The Marxists have also made a great mistake. They totally failed to see the rise of the American militia movement. And they have not developed an armed revolutionary force of their own. And they totally missed the rise of the Christian Fundamentalist type of Christianity. This is actually a political force.

アメリカのマルクス主義者たちは、一つの大きな間違いをしました。まず、アメリカの民兵組織が増加することを全く考慮していませんでした。一方、彼らには、自分たちの革命軍というものがありません。さらに、キリスト教原理主義が台頭してくることを、全く考えていませんでした。実は、これら二つの組織は非常に政治的な

67

Chapter2 The true roots of Political Correctness

権力を持ったグループなのです。

So by so many violent protests against President Trump, the Marxist Left in America is setting the stage for violent Civil War. And they will lose this badly, many will die.

トランプ大統領に対して暴力的な抗議をすることで、マルクス主義の左派たちは、アメリカにおける暴力的な内乱のお膳立てをしています。ですが、こうした左派は大敗し、数多くの人が死ぬでしょう。

But America will be devastated.

しかし、アメリカは荒廃してしまいます。

There is so much hate in America. In 2004, I was a volunteer in Japan to register Americans to vote in the Presidential election. It was John Kerry versus George Bush. So many Americans told me "I hate John

John Kerry vs. George Bush
ジョン・ケリーとジョージ・ブッシュ

Kerry" or "I hate George Bush". Now for me, I could say I do not respect George Bush, and I voted against him, but I could never say "hate".

　現在アメリカには、それだけの嫌悪感、憎しみがあるのです。2004年、私は、アメリカ人が日本で大統領選挙に投票できるよう登録するボランティアでした。その時の選挙は、ジョン・ケリー氏対ジョージ・W・ブッシュ氏でした。私は数多くのアメリカ人から「私はジョン・ケリーが嫌いだ」あるいは「私はジョージ・ブッシュが嫌いだ」という声を聞きました。私の場合、「ジョージ・ブッシュを尊敬していない」「彼には投票しない」と言うことはできますが、「嫌いだ（ヘイト）」という言葉は、絶対に使いません。

You see, for Americans, hate is only one step away from killing someone. And that is why America is close to Civil War.

　アメリカ人にとって嫌悪感（ヘイト）というのは、人を殺す一歩手前です。だからこそ、アメリカには内乱が近いと言えるのです。

The scary Feminist movement
恐るべきフェミニスト集団

Let us take a look at this hate. I will now include same Feminist indoctrination from an article I found on the net. The article is titled "Marxist Feminism's Ruined Lives" written by Mallory Millett.

　この嫌悪感、ヘイトという感情について、さらに見てみましょう。以下に、私がネットで見つけた「フェミニストの教え」を書きます。マロリー・ミレット氏が書いた記事、"Marxist Feminism's Ruined Lives"（マルクス主義のフェミニズムによる堕落した人生）からの引用です。

Chapter2 The true roots of Political Correctness

This is a Feminist meeting in an apartment in New York. The person identified as "she" is the leader. The people identified as "they" are the group of about a dozen people.

これは、ニューヨーク市にあるアパートでの、フェミニストたちの集会の様子です。「彼女」と呼ばれている人は、この人たちのリーダーです。「彼女たち」と呼ばれているのは、集会に集まったメンバーたちです。

Quote from the article.

記事から引用：

"Why are we here today?" she asked.

「私たちはなぜ今日、ここにいるの？」彼女が聞く。

"To make revolution," they answered.

「革命を起こすために」彼女たちが答える。

"What kind of revolution?" she replied.

「それはどんな革命？」彼女が言う。

"The Cultural Revolution," they chanted.

「文化の革命」彼女たちが唱和する。

"And how do we make Cultural Revolution?" she demanded.

「どうやって文化に革命を起こすの？」彼女が問いただす。

70

第 2 章　ポリティカル・コレクトネスの本当のルーツ

"By destroying the American family!" they answered.

「アメリカ家庭の破壊によって！」彼女たちが答える。

"How do we destroy the family?" she came back.

「では、どうやって家庭を破壊するの？」彼女が聞き返す。

"By destroying the American Patriarch," they cried exuberantly.

「アメリカの家長制度を破壊することによって！」彼女たちが力強く叫ぶ。

"And how do we destroy the American Patriarch?" she replied.

「では、どうやってアメリカの家長制度を破壊するの？」彼女が言う。

"By taking away his power!"

「男たちから権力を奪い去ることによって！」

"How do we do that?"

「どうやって？」

"By destroying monogamy!" they shouted.

「一夫一婦制の破壊によって！」彼女たちが叫ぶ。

"How can we destroy monogamy?"

「一夫一婦制をどうやって破壊するの？」

71

Chapter2 The true roots of Political Correctness

"By promoting promiscuity, eroticism, prostitution and homosexuality!" they resounded.

「乱交、好色、売春、同性愛を奨励することによって！」彼女たちの歓声が響きわたった。

Unquote

引用終わり

Now notice how much this meeting is like religious indoctrination as practiced in more authoritarian religions in the West. Also notice how they do not offer any kind of idea of what society they wish to construct. They only talk of destroying present society.

この集会は、まるで西洋の権威主義的な宗教の教化と同じであるということに注目してください。それと、破壊のあとにどのような社会を作りたいのかという提案がない、ということにも気がつくでしょう。彼らは、現在の社会を破壊するという話しかしていないのです。

In the above meeting, the term Patriarch means American men. The goal of Feminists is to completely destroy American men.

上記の集会で、「家長制度」という言葉が指しているのは、アメリカの男性たちのことです。フェミニストたちの目標は、アメリカの男性を完全に滅ぼすことなのです。

In a previous book, "The truth about Americans", I have written how American men think of Japan as a "Candy Store" They go crazy over Japanese women, and often make fools of themselves.

私が以前書いた本『アメリカ人の本音』(桜の花出版、2014年)に、アメリカの男性が日本のことを「キャンディーストア（お菓子屋さ

ん）」と考えている、ということを書きました。彼らは日本の女性に夢中になり、よく自分自身のことを笑いものにします。

Well, when you consider that Feminist meeting, and the attitudes of American women towards men, it is not surprising. Japanese women are women. They are feminine, dress well, and treat men with respect.

まあ、先ほどのフェミニスト集会を知ったあとなら、アメリカ男性に対するアメリカ女性の態度を実際に見ても、さほど驚かないでしょう。日本の女性は、まさに女性です。彼女たちは女性らしく、きちんとした服を着て、男性に敬意をもって接します。

About 18% of American women can be considered Feminists. They tend to be concentrated in big cities, and voted for Clinton in the election.

アメリカ女性の 18%はフェミニストであると考えられています。だいたいは大都市に集中していて、この前の大統領選挙でクリントン氏に投票した人たちです。

Why Americans tried to change Japan by provoking war
アメリカが日本を戦争に引きずり込んだ理由

The American Left are a group of spoiled children. There is a new term on the American Right for such advocates of extreme political correctness, such people are called "delicate snowflakes".

アメリカの左派は、まるで甘やかされた子供です。こうした極端なポリティカル・コレクトネスを唱道している人たちに対して、アメリカの右派が作った新しい言葉があります。それは "delicate snowflakes"（壊れやすい雪片）という言葉です。

That is because every snowflake is said to be of a unique individual

Chapter2 The true roots of Political Correctness

design. But with their constant provocations to radically change American society, these "delicate snowflakes" will create a firestorm from hell in America. They will not survive it.

雪片は、それぞれが独特な形をしているから、というのが、その理由です。しかし、彼らの急進的かつ徹底的にアメリカ社会を変化させようとする扇動によって、この「壊れやすい雪片」は、まるで地獄のような炎の嵐を作ります。でも彼らは、そこで生き残ることはできないでしょう。

Americans try too much to make a perfect world with no prejudice. They cannot live with people as they are. They don't understand this fact because Americans do not have history. By trying to force change, inevitably they resort to violence, and mass killing. That is why Americans forced Japan into WWII, into attacking Pearl Harbor.

アメリカ人は、いつも、完璧に差別がない社会を創ろうとします。彼らは、「生まれたそのまま」で共存することができません。アメリカには歴史がないから、この真実を理解できないのです。そして、強制的に他国民を変化させようとするので、必然的に、暴力や大虐殺に向かってしまうのです。それが、日本を大東亜戦争に引きずりこんだ理由でもあります。

They could not live with Japan as it is. First they felt they must destroy Japan, then they felt they must change Japan. Even today they still celebrate the war as changing Japan, even though they did not really succeed in changing Japan so much. They are still attempting to change Japan into something the same as America. But the effort will fail, because they destroy themselves.

彼らは当時、「ありのままの日本」と共存することができませんでした。そこで、まず最初は、日本を破壊しなければならないと感じました。その次に、日本を変化させなければならないと感じまし

第 2 章　ポリティカル・コレクトネスの本当のルーツ

た。現在でも彼らは、日本を変えたあの戦争を祝福しています。た
とえ、実際には日本をそれほど変えることができなかったとしても。
その上、今でも日本を、アメリカと同じような国に変化させようと
しています。しかし、それは必ず失敗するでしょう。なぜなら、ア
メリカ自身が自滅するからです。

Americans, cannot co-exist with Japan, or any other nation, they also
cannot co-exist with themselves. And they are destroying their nation over
trivial issues. They call this political correctness.

アメリカ人は、日本だけでなく、その他のどの国とも共存するこ
とができません。それどころか、自分の国の中でも共存することが
できていません。ささいなことを問題にして、自分の国を破壊して
います。彼らはこれを、ポリティカル・コレクトネスと呼びます。

Chapter 3
America the ignorant
無知なアメリカ

The destruction of the American education system
崩壊するアメリカの教育システム

We have seen the damage that political correctness has done to University education in America. But what about American high school, middle school and primary school education? Let us take a look.

ここまで何度か、いかにポリティカル・コレクトネスがアメリカの大学レベルの教育にダメージを与えているかということを見てきました。では、アメリカの小中高の教育はどうでしょうか？ 次に、それを見てみましょう。

There can be no denying that American education is in shambles. How did this happen? After all, in the period after World War Two, America led the world in scientific achievement. America's education system, in particular the University system, was admired by all.

アメリカの教育システムが、めちゃくちゃなことは事実です。しかし、いったいどうして、こうなってしまったのでしょうか？ 第二次世界大戦後、アメリカは科学技術の成果によって、世界をリードしてきました。そして、アメリカの教育システム、特に、アメリカの大学制度が、世界中から注目を集めていました。

I think one root cause was the abdication of authority by American

第3章　無知なアメリカ

educators. I saw this in my own high school. Partly what caused this was the Vietnam war protests.

　アメリカの教育システムが崩壊した大きな原因の一つは、アメリカの教育者たちが、その権威を放棄してしまったことでしょう。私は、自分の高等学校で、実際にそれを見ました。部分的な理由には、ベトナム戦争への抗議もあったでしょう。

Those protests shook American society to it's core. People began to doubt what had been regarded as traditional American values.

　ベトナム戦争に対する抗議活動は、アメリカ社会の中心部にまで深い影響を与えました。人々は、それまでのアメリカの伝統的な価値観を疑い始めました。

Also, since America is a new country, many people love new scientific theory, especially psychiatry. Many psychiatrists made careers for themselves by recommending new ways of education.

　アメリカは新しい国ですから、そこに住む人々も、新しい科学、特に精神医学の分野が好きです。そのため、多くの精神科医が新しい教育の方法を考え出し、それによって自分の地位を築きました。

In general, these theories said discipline was bad, children should be consulted and asked what they wanted to learn.

　こうした新しい理論は、一般的に、古い規律が悪いとか、子供たち自身に何を勉強したいか聞くべきだ、というような話ばかりでした。

I remember this at my high school in Wisconsin. The principal gathered all the students in an assembly and asked, what did we want to study. The reply was guitar playing and macrame. Macrame is the weaving colorful designs out of yarn.

　私が通っていたウィスコンシン州の高等学校で、こんなことが

77

Chapter3 America the ignorant

あったのを覚えています。ある時、校長先生が生徒を全員集めて、皆に、何を勉強したいですかと尋ねました。それに対する学生たちの返事は、「ギターの弾き方」と「マクラメ」でした。マクラメというのは、織り糸を使って、カラフルなデザインの小物を作ることです。

Nobody wanted to study science, mathematics, history, english language or any foreign language. Well, I wanted to study these things.

科学、数学、歴史、英語や外国語を勉強したいという生徒など、一人もいませんでした。まあ、私自身には、そういうことを勉強したいという気持ちがありましたが。

In my high school, people studied Spanish because it was easy, the teacher was a joke, people always took the easiest course. What I mean here by the teacher was a joke, he always gave passing grades, no matter how bad the student's work was. He even had tequila parties in class.

私の高校では、スペイン語が楽勝科目だからという理由で、皆がそれを選びました。先生は変わった人でした。その先生はテストの点数がどんなにひどくても、生徒に合格点を出しました。それと、メキシコの文化を教えるためだといって、クラスでテキーラ・パーティーを開催しました。

Well, of course, high school students are not legally allowed to drink alcohol, he got fired for that.

もちろん、高校生は未成年者ですから、その飲酒パーティーで先生は解雇されました。

And the truth is, Americans have always had some kind of feeling that even ignorant of facts, somehow American common sense would prevail.

もう一つの真実として、アメリカ人というのは、人がどんなに無

78

第3章　無知なアメリカ

知であろうとも、常識さえあれば勝てる、頑張れる、何とかなる、と信じているのです。

The Sam Cooke song, "Wonderful world", popular in the 1960's, illustrates this. The lyrics go something like: I don't know mathematics or history, or anything, but I know I love you.

1960年代のサム・クック氏の曲、「ワンダフル・ワールド」を聞けば、彼らのこの信念が分かります。歌詞は、こんな感じです。「僕は、数学も、歴史も、何も知らない。だけど、『アイ・ラブ・ユー』を知っている」

Well, if a person does not know anything, how can he get a decent job and raise a family?

だけど、ある人が本当に何も知らないとして、どうやってまともな仕事について、どうやって家族を養っていくのでしょうか？

Feminists alter history education
フェミニストによる歴史教育への介入

But if I may point out one major cause of education failure in America, I would have to say it is because the overwhelming majority of American school teachers are women.

しかし、アメリカ教育の崩壊の原因の一つとして、私は、大多数のアメリカの学校の先生が女性だということを挙げたいと思います。

As the women's liberation movement gained importance after the Vietnam war, these women decided to use education as a tool for social change, from the primary school level up.

Chapter3 America the ignorant

　ベトナム戦争後に始まった女性解放運動（ウーマン・リブ）が、だんだんと力を増し、こうしたフェミニストたちが、社会を変えるために、小学校レベルから教育を利用することを決めたのです。

How did this work? First of all, let us talk about the American Civil war. Let us consider five historical people. Abraham Lincoln, Ulysses S Grant, Jefferson Davis, Robert E. Lee, and Harriet Tubman.

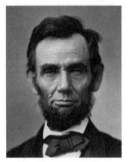

Abraham Lincoln
エイブラハム・リンカーン

Ulysses S. Grant
ユリシーズ・グラント

Jefferson Davis
ジェファーソン・デイヴィス

Robert E. Lee
ロバート・E・リー

第 3 章　無知なアメリカ

　それは、どのように実行されたのでしょうか？　まず、アメリカ
の南北戦争をテーマにして考えてみましょう。ここでは、5人の歴
史上の人物を取り上げてみます。それは、エイブラハム・リンカー
ン氏、ユリシーズ・グラント氏、ジェファーソン・デイヴィス氏、
ロバート・E・リー氏、そして、黒人女性であるハリエット・タブ
マン氏です。

Abraham Lincoln was the President of the Northern States.　Ulysses S.
Grant was at the end of the war the Commander in chief of the Northern
armies, and later a President of the United States.　Jefferson Davis was the
President of the Southern states, the Confederacy.　Robert E. Lee was the
greatest general the South had.

　エイブラハム・リンカーン氏は、北部の州の大統領でした。ユリ
シーズ・グラント氏は北軍の総司令官を務めた将軍で、その後はア
メリカ大統領にもなりました。ジェファーソン・デイヴィス氏はア
メリカ連合国、つまり南部の州の大統領でした。ロバート・E・リー
氏は、南軍の最も偉大な将軍でした。

Harriet Tubman was an escaped slave from the South, who led many
other Black slaves to freedom on secret escape routes from the South to
the North.

　一方のハリエット・タブマン女史は、南部から逃亡した奴隷であ
り、秘密の逃亡ルートを使って、南から北の自由州へ、数多くの奴
隷を逃がしました。

Now I remember that Harriet Tubman was mentioned in my textbook in
high school about the American Civil War.　But let us consider something.
She was a very minor figure in that war.　Yes, what she did was very brave
and heroic.

　私も、自分の高校時代の教科書に、ハリエット・タブマン氏のこ

81

Chapter3 America the ignorant

とが書かれていたのを覚えています。しかし、ちょっと考えてみてください。確かに、彼女は勇敢な英雄です。でも、南北戦争における役割としては、彼女は小さな、マイナーな役割を演じたに過ぎません。

But the decisions taken by those first four men, shaped events. Harriet Tubman reacted to those events. But she did not, and could not, decide the fate of either nation, The United States of America or the Confederate States of America.

実際に歴史を動かしていたのは、先に取り上げた4人の男たちです。ハリエット・タブマン氏は、彼らの作った歴史の中で、確かに、ある役割を演じました。しかし彼女は、アメリカ合衆国、アメリカ連合国、どちらの国に対しても、その運命を決めるようなことまで

Harriet Tubman

ハリエット・タブマン

は、できませんでした。

Yet in today's social climate in America, the overwhelming emphasis in school would be on Harriet Tubman and other people like her. She is a double bonus, she was Black and a woman.

それでも、現在のアメリカの教育現場では、ハリエット・タブマン氏のような女性の話が、大々的に取り上げられるのです。彼女は、いわゆる「ダブル・ボーナス」です。つまり、女性でもあり、黒人でもあるからです。

Another aspect of the problem of having so many women as teachers is the Feminist movement, and the Feminization of the American male.

多くの学校の先生が女性であることの、もう一つの問題は、フェミニスト運動の増進と、アメリカ男性の女性化です。

Feminist philosophy teaches that all the world's problems are caused by competitive men. So their thinking goes, if competition and male spirit were eliminated, so would world conflict be eliminated.

フェミニスト哲学の教えによれば、すべての世界の問題の原因は、競争的な男どもにある、ということです。そして、もしも競争意識と男性的なものをこの世からなくすことができれば、世界に平和が訪れると考えているのです。

The drugging of American students
クスリづけにされる子供たち

Thus we have the mass drugging of American school children. On any given day, some 2 million American children are drugged by their schools. These are drugs such as Ritalin. Americans like to have new ideas.

Chapter3 America the ignorant

Psychiatry is beloved by Americans. Being a new country, they think that new ideas will solve all problems.

　それで今、学校に通う子供たちを精神安定剤でおとなしくさせる、というような事態が起こっています。だいたい、毎日、学校で 200 万人の生徒が精神安定剤を飲んでいるといいます。中でもリタリンという安定剤は人気です。前にも言ったように、アメリカ人は、新しい提案が好きです。精神医学も愛されています。アメリカは新しい国ですから、新しいアイディアでどんな問題でも解決できると信じているのです。

So psychiatrists have invented many types of new mental disorders, such as Attention Deficit Disorder, or Hyper Activity Syndrome. And many others.

　それで、精神医学の学者たちが、新しい精神的な病気をいっぱい考え出します。例えば、注意欠陥障害や注意欠陥多動性障害など、その他にもいっぱいあります。

When I was a kid, it was natural that children would not pay attention, and want to run around and play physically. The teachers would force us to concentrate on our schoolwork by the power of their personalities.

　私が子供のころなど、子供が集中できずに、あちこち走り回ったりするのは、自然なことでした。それを、先生が、自分たちの能力を使って、勉強に集中するようにさせていたのです。

I had a teacher who could get students to pay attention in high school. He was the Algebra teacher. He was also the football coach.

　私の通っていた高校にも、そうした、生徒を上手く集中させることができる先生がいました。彼は数学（代数）の先生でした。また、彼はアメリカン・フットボールのコーチでもありました。

第 3 章　無知なアメリカ

I hated mathematics, and never did well in any math class. Except Algebra. I remember falling asleep in class one day. Suddenly WHAM! The blackboard eraser hit me in the head! It was thrown by the teacher, who was of course the football coach, and could hit anything directly.

当時、私は数学が大嫌いでしたし、実際、数学のクラスでは、いつも成績が悪かったです。ただし、代数だけは上手くいきました。今でも覚えているのですが、ある日の授業中、居眠りをしている私の頭に、突然「ドーン！」と黒板消しが当たりました！　先生はアメフトのコーチなので、何にでも投げて当てることができたのです。

I got very good grades in that class, because he motivated me to work hard.

私は、その代数のクラスで良い点数を取りました。その先生が私を、もっと頑張ろうという気持ちにさせてくれたからです。

But in today's politically correct climate, he would be fired for doing such a thing.

でも、現在のポリティカル・コレクトネスの風潮では、その先生はすぐに解雇されてしまうでしょう。

However, in 2016, a professor at Queens college in New York stated that Algebra should no longer be taught. Andrew Hacker, the teacher said because it is so difficult, students drop out of school. If it was no longer taught, more students would graduate from school.

2016 年、ニューヨーク市立大学クイーンズ校の教授が、学校では代数を教えない方がいいと言い出しました。アンドリュー・ハッカー先生によれば、代数が難しいために、数多くの学生が学校から中退するということです。だから、もし代数を教えなくなれば、卒業する学生が増えるというのです。

Chapter3 America the ignorant

Just a minute here. This teacher cannot teach. So then difficult courses should be dropped? Algebra is basic high school mathematics. After that is Geometry, then Trigonometry and Calculus. Without mathematically educated people, how can America maintain itself as a country with any sort of technology? My high school teacher certainly had much more personal power, and teaching ability, than this professor.

でも、ちょっと待ってください。この先生に教える能力がないからといって、難しい勉強をあきらめてしまうのですか？ 代数は、数学の基礎です。その次には幾何学や三角法や微分積分が控えています。国民に数学が教育されていない状態で、どうやってアメリカはテクノロジーを維持するのでしょうか。私の高校の先生は、この大学の先生よりも、心の力、人に何かを教える能力がありました。

It seems that modern American teachers lack such personal power. So they rely on drugs to control children.

やはり、現在のアメリカ人の先生にそのような心の力がないから、生徒たちを支配するために、精神安定剤を利用するのでしょう。

These drugs turn children into quiet, obedient zombies. They also have many long term bad effects, such as turning the children into drug dependent people.

こうしたクスリを使えば、確かに子供はおとなしく、従順なゾンビになります。しかし、長期間こうした安定剤を飲めば、悪い影響もたくさん出ます。例えば、将来、このような薬物に依存する人になる可能性が高くなるでしょう。

This drugging is involuntary. The parents of the children have no voice in the matter. The teachers themselves decide who gets drugged. If the parents do not like it, they must remove their children from school.

この安定剤を飲むことが不本意であろうと、子供の親には選択権

86

第3章　無知なアメリカ

がありません。先生だけが、誰に安定剤を飲ませるかを決めます。もし子供の親がその安定剤を飲ませることに反対の場合、子供を学校から引き揚げるしか方法がないのです。

It is very likely that major American Pharmaceutical firms have a big role in this. If TPP had been approved, they would have likely done the same thing in Japanese schools.

アメリカの巨大な製薬会社が、この問題の背後で大きな役割を演じているのかもしれません。もし TPP を日本が認めていたら、日本の学校でも同じようなことが起こったでしょう。

Overly sensitive students
あまりにも敏感な学生

American students today are incredibly weak of heart and sensitive. In high school and university, there is a new concept called, "trigger alerts". What is this?

現在のアメリカの学生は、信じられないくらい敏感で、心の弱い人たちです。高等学校と大学には、「トリガー警告」というものがあります。これは何でしょう?

Well, when the teacher is about to bring up a subject that may upset students, he or she have to warn them that they may be upset by the material.

これは、先生が学生たちに動揺する可能性のあることを教える場合、あらかじめ、その授業の内容で彼らが動揺するかもしれないと注意してもらうことです。

87

Chapter3 America the ignorant

For example, A teacher teaching Latin literature had problems with the poem "Ovid". It is a classic of Latin literature, in it the Goddess Proserpina is raped.

例えば、ローマ帝国の文学を教える先生が授業で使った、オービッド（オウィディウス）の詩が問題になりました。これはローマ帝国の文学の古典なのですが、その詩では、女神プロセルピナがレイプされます。

But many students, particularly young women, feel very uncomfortable hearing this story. So Universities provide "safe spaces". I have read about one such safe space at Brown University.

しかし、数多くの学生、特に女子学生が、この話を聞いて不快な気持ちを持ちました。そこで大学は「安全な場所」というところを作りました。私は、アメリカのブラウン大学で、この「安全な場所」に関する説明を読んだことがあります。

A speaker was coming to the school to challenge the concept of the phrase "rape culture". The phrase "rape culture" means any cultural aspect that women find insulting. It can mean any word or picture that a particular person finds insulting. They feel that it is the same as rape. Well the truth is rape is forced sex against the will of a person. It is not an insult, or a picture someone does not like. But the American left, and university population, have become way too sensitive.

ある評論家が、「レイプ文化（レイプ・カルチャー）」という考え方に異議を唱えるために、ある講演会に参加しました。「レイプ文化」という言葉の意味は、女性が社会的な面で失礼な扱いを受けるということであり、例えば、ある言葉や写真などを失礼だと感じた場合、それはレイプと同じだという考え方です。でも、レイプというのは、嫌がる人に無理やり肉体的なセックスを強要することであり、失礼な言葉や嫌いな写真とは違います。でもアメリカの左派、特に大学

88

第3章　無知なアメリカ

の先生と学生たちは、こうしたことに過度に敏感です。

Any kind of touch, or even just a look, can now be interpreted as rape or attempted rape. Americans, particularly Feminists, are developing a victim complex, that is ridiculous.

ほんの少し人に触れること、ほんの少し視線を合わせることが、現在の社会では、レイプかレイプ未遂のように受け取られるのです。アメリカ人、特にフェミニストが、こうした馬鹿げた犠牲者コンプレックスを促進しています。

In any case, the described "safe space" had cookies, play-doh, coloring books, and counselors for students who did not want to attend the lecture. One student who used the "safe space" said that she attended the event briefly, but since the debate challenged her deep set beliefs, she quickly retreated to the "safe space".

とにかく、この「安全な場所」には、クッキーや子供用の粘土、ぬり絵の本があり、授業に出たくない学生のためのカウンセラーも待機していました。ここを利用する女子学生の一人は、あるイベントに少しだけ参加したところ、自分の信念とは反対のことが語られていたので、すぐにこの「安全な場所」へと逃げ帰ったそうです。

Brown University is an elite college on the American East Coast, and described in a New York Times article.

このブラウン大学というのは、アメリカ東海岸にあるエリート大学です。私は、ニューヨーク・タイムズの記事で、このことを読みました。

89

Chapter3 America the ignorant

An education in self esteem
自尊心ばかりを持ち上げる教育

Also, students panic and freak out if given bad grades. When I was a high school student, if I got bad grades, the teacher would tell me it was because I did not study hard enough. That was correct.

また、こういう問題もあります。もしも良い成績が取れなかった場合、学生たちがパニックを起こし、異常な精神状態になる、というのです。私が高校生の時に、もし成績が悪ければ、先生は私に「君は勉強が足りない」と言ったでしょう。それはまさに、正しい指摘です。

Today, many university and high school teachers give good grades no matter how bad the work is. This is because it is too much trouble for the teachers to deal with students who do poorly.

でも、現在の多くの学校の先生の場合、学生がどんなにひどい点数であろうとも、合格の成績を出すでしょう。理由は、出来の悪い学生に教えることは、面倒くさくて大変だからです。

So we end up with people graduating from school who have learned nothing.

結局、学校からは、何も学んでない学生たちが卒業していくことになります。

And students grade their teachers. They actually rank their teachers, these rankings are given to the school administrators. The administrators then base employment of teachers on the rankings.

また、アメリカでは、学生が先生に評点をつけます。実際、彼ら

第3章　無知なアメリカ

は先生のランキング表を作って、学校の経営者に渡します。そして、経営者がその先生の雇用を続けるかどうかの判断に、こうした学生のランキングが強い影響を与えるのです。

There is something extremely wrong with this. By definition, students are ignorant, and need instruction to learn. Teachers are those with knowledge and experience who provide instruction and guidance for students.

これは、ひどい間違いです。はっきり言って、学生というのは、無知で、教育が必要な人たちです。一方、教師は、経験と知識を持っている人で、学生に教育と指導を与える人です。

If we give such great power to students, we create arrogant monsters, not well educated adults.

大きすぎる力を学生に与えると、教育された大人ではなく、傲慢なモンスターを作ります。

Another horrible result of the emphasis on non competition is the elevation of self esteem education. Competition produces a better person. You gain this by the bitter experience of losing, and finding pain. The pain leads to overcome the problem, and you emerge as a stronger individual.

もう一つ、競争を避ける教育が招く恐ろしい結果は、自尊心ばかりを持ち上げるような教育になってしまう、ということです。競争は、良い人格を作ります。もちろん、競争に負けるという経験は苦しいです。しかし、この心の痛みによって、人はさらに努力して、もっと強い人間になるのです。

If you teach constant self esteem, children begin to believe they are wonderful as they are. Then there is no need to make any effort to improve or to learn something.

91

Chapter3 America the ignorant

　自尊心ばかりを教えると、子供は、自分たちはそのままで素晴らしいのだと考えるようになります。ならば、何かを学んで、もっと良くなるように努力することは、必要なくなってしまいます。

Why? Because they have been taught that they are already perfect.

なぜなら彼らは「そのままで完璧だよ」と教えられているからです。

Immature adults
大人だけど幼稚な人々

This is one reason Americans are so poor at learning languages or international business. Since they are the greatest people in the world, everybody should learn English to please them.

　これは、アメリカ人が他国の言語を習うこと、あるいは国際ビジネスが苦手な理由の一つです。自分たちアメリカ人が世界で最も素晴らしいのだから、他国の人たちはアメリカ人を喜ばせるために英語を覚えるべきだ、というわけです。

Since their ideas are the greatest in the world, people should naturally buy their products. They simply cannot comprehend the need to study another culture to try understand what people truly desire.

　同様に、アメリカ人のアイディアは世界で最も優れているのだから、自然に世界中の人々がアメリカ人の作った品物を買うだろうと思っています。だから、他国の人のニーズを知るためには、他国の文化を勉強する必要がある、ということを全く理解できません。

When their products do not sell, they suspect some plot or hidden barrier is preventing the product from selling. After all, school has taught them that they are perfect as they are, no need to improve. Then they threaten

92

第 3 章　無知なアメリカ

violence with the United States military.

　彼らの作った品物が売れない時には、秘密の陰謀か、隠れた障壁
があると考えます。まあ、彼らは学校で、自分たちは完璧であり、
改善などする必要はないと習っていますから。それで、最後には、
他国を米軍の暴力で脅かします。

A very childish reaction.

実に子供っぽい反応です。

So what the present American educational system is producing is
over sensitive egotistical people, who may be chronologically adult, but
have infantile minds. They cannot take any kind of hardship, and expect
immediate success as their right.

　このように、現在のアメリカの教育システムは、過度に敏感で、
自分勝手な人間を作り続けています。彼らは、年齢的には大人です
が、精神的にはとても幼稚です。彼らはどんな苦労も我慢すること
ができず、すぐに成功できることだけを望んでいます。

So when their preferred candidate, Hillary Clinton lost her bid to
become President, the young American Left people rioted, they threw a
childish temper tantrum. Many others could be seen collapsed on the floor
in public places such as airports. They simply could not perform normal
things like walking and sitting up straight.

　アメリカの左派の若者が大好きな大統領候補、ヒラリー・クリン
トン氏が落選した時、彼らが暴動を起こしましたが、これも、実の
ところは子供の癇癪に過ぎません。公共の場、例えば空港で、多く
の若者が床に寝ころがっていましたが、普通のこと、例えば、歩い
たり、まっすぐに座ったりするということができないのでしょう。

Well, all their life in school they have been taught they will achieve

93

Chapter3 America the ignorant

satisfaction by simply showing up. They have not experienced loss, they don't know how to deal with it. So they reacted like spoiled children.

　まあ、彼らが生まれてから学校で教えられてきたことといえば、ただ何かに参加するだけで満足が得られるようなことばかりです。彼らには負けた経験がないから、負けた時にどうすればいいのか、その方法が分かりません。それで、甘やかされた子供のような反応をしたわけです。

Selfish foreigners living in Japan
日本に暮らすワガママな外国人

There is a new word in America for these spoiled people, they are called "Special Snowflakes". That is because every actual snowflake has a unique shape. But the truth is that such people are extremely difficult to work with.

　先ほど私は、アメリカではこういう甘やかされた人を指す新しい単語があり、それは「特別な雪片」と呼ばれていると言いました。理由は、雪片はそれぞれに独特の形を持っているから、ということでしたね。しかし、実際、こういう人たちを仕事で使うことは、とても大変です。

I had many experiences with such spoiled Americans when I worked in the Japanese talent business. I worked for an office that would supply foreigner actors and extras for Japanese television and film.

　かつて私が日本のタレント業界で働いていて、こういう甘やかされたアメリカ人たちと仕事をした際に、そうした経験をたくさんしました。当時、私の事務所は、日本のテレビ番組、映画などのために、外国人の役者やエキストラを派遣していました。

第3章　無知なアメリカ

All too often, the Americans were very selfish and demanding. They were paid on the average 3 times what a Japanese person was paid. Yet they wanted special foods, or a special room to wait in, or many other things.

ほとんどのアメリカ人は、非常にワガママで、数多くの要求をしました。基本的に、彼らのギャラは日本人の3倍でした。しかも、特別な食事、特別な控え室、その他、数多くのことを要求しました。

They would rarely show up for a job on time. And another thing that always angered me was they tried to take photos with the Japanese star of any production we were filming in. This is a very rude thing, no Japanese person would do that.

彼らが時間通りに仕事に来ることは、めずらしいことでした。もう一つ、私を怒らせたことは、彼らは常に、その撮影で一緒になる日本人スターと写真を撮ろうとしたことです。これは、本当に失礼なことで、日本人はこのようなことを絶対にしません。

When I would inform the foreigner that such behavior was not liked in Japan, usually they would reply, "Well the show wants foreigners, this is how foreigners behave!".

私がそうした外国人たちに、そのような態度は日本では認められないということを教えると、ほとんどの外国人は、こう言い返します。「この番組は外国人が欲しいんだろう？　だったらこれが、外国人のやり方だ！」

Eventually, I got disgusted with such foreigners and quit that business. Today, almost no foreigners are used anymore in Japanese films.

だんだん私は、そういう外国人たちに嫌気がさして、その業界を辞めてしまいました。現在では、日本の映画で外国人を使うことが、めずらしくなりました。

95

Chapter3 America the ignorant

No wonder America is in such a mess, becoming a failed state.

だから私には、現在のめちゃくちゃな状態のアメリカ、間もなく失敗国家になるアメリカにも、驚きはないのです。

As for myself, the greatest educational experience I had was Marine Corps "Boot Camp", or basic training.

私自身に関して言えば、私にとって一番役に立った教育経験は、「ブートキャンプ」、つまり海兵隊の新兵訓練所でした。

The Marines are very strict in the training of new Marines. This is because Marines are expected to go into very difficult and dangerous situations, and win.

海兵隊は、新兵の訓練に対して、とても厳しいです。なぜなら海兵隊は、非常に苦しい、危険な場所へ行って、戦闘に勝つことが当たり前だからです。

This is not torture as most Americans think. It is very carefully calibrated to get you to make strong effort, to the most of your ability, and beyond.

多くのアメリカ人が考えているものと違い、これは拷問ではありません。この訓練によって新兵が強く努力できるように、また、自分の能力の限界まで、さらにそれ以上に頑張れるように、注意深く調整されている訓練なのです。

Marines are trained to deal with reality, no matter how harsh it may be.

どんなに過酷な事態にあっても、海兵隊がその問題に対処できるよう、彼らは訓練されているのです。

America does not have enough Marines.

だからこそ、アメリカでは今、海兵隊の数が足りません。

96

What is Christian Fundamentalism
キリスト教原理主義とは何か

Oh and before I forget. I must write about religious schooling. No, I don't mean Catholic schools. I mean Christian Fundamentalist schools. Basically they teach that the Bible is literally correct, every word is absolute truth.

さて、ここで忘れてはいけないのが、宗教教育のことです。これを書かないとダメです。これは、単にカトリックの学校の話ではありません。キリスト教原理主義の学校について、私は書きたいのです。基本的に、こうした学校においては、聖書に書かれている事は完全に正しい、どんな言葉も一字一句、完璧に真実であると教えられます。

Two states in America, permit such teaching in the public schools, Louisiana and Tennessee. But such teaching exists in schools in other states.

アメリカでは、二つの州、ルイジアナ州とテネシー州で、公立学校においてキリスト教原理主義の教育を許可しています。しかし、他の州にも、そうした学校はあります。

What sort of things do they teach? Well, they teach that the earth is about 6,000 years old. This is the Usher chronology, developed by the Archbishop of Armagh county in Ireland in the 17th century.

こうした学校では、どのようなことを教えるのでしょうか？　まず、地球が出来たのは6千年前であると教えます。これは「アッシャーの年表」によるもので、アッシャーは17世紀アイルランドのアーマー州の大司教でした。

Chapter3 America the ignorant

They teach that before Eve ate from the apple, dinosaurs and humans lived together peacefully, and that the dinosaurs were all peaceful vegetarians.

彼らはこう教えます。イブがリンゴを食べる前には、恐竜と人間が仲良く共同生活をしていました。恐竜は皆、優しくて菜食主義でした。

Christian museums have dioramas showing Adam living together with a vegetarian T-Rex. When Eve ate from the apple, the dinosaurs became sinful, and meat eaters.

キリスト原理主義の博物館に展示されたジオラマでは、アダムと菜食主義のティラノサウルスが、一緒に暮らしています。イブがリンゴを食べたので、恐竜たちも罪深い生きものとなり、肉食になりました。

The dinosaurs were wiped out in the Great Flood. The Great Flood also carved out the American Grand Canyon, instantly. It is not hundreds of millions of years old.

恐竜たちは、大洪水によって絶滅しました。この大洪水は、アメリカのグランドキャニオンを一瞬で作りました。何億年もかかってできたというのは、嘘です。

These are some of the things that are taught as scientific fact in such schools. Children brought up and educated in such a system will have an extremely difficult time in a normal university.

上記は、キリスト教原理主義の学校で教えられている科学的な真実です。そういう学校と教えの中で育った子供が普通の大学に入学したら、とても大変でしょう。

In a recent Gallup poll, in 2012, it was found that 46% of Americans

第 3 章　無知なアメリカ

believe in such creation science.

　でも、2012 年のギャラップ世論調査で、46％のアメリカ人がこ
うした創造科学を信じていることが明らかになっています。

Many people in Japan hope for me to explain the truth of the Japanese
role in the The Great Pacific War. But how can I explain, for example,
the truth about Comfort Women, when the American education system is
turning out such ignorant monsters, who think they know everything, and
ignore that which they do not like?

　先述のように、日本では、数多くの人が私に、アメリカ人に対し
て大東亜戦争の真実を説明してほしいと思っています。しかし、ア
メリカの教育システムがこのように、自分は何でも知っていると考
え、自分が嫌いな話は無視し、無知なモンスターを作り出している
中で、例えば、慰安婦問題の真実を、どう説明したらいいのでしょ
うか？

Chapter 4
The problem of race in America
アメリカの人種問題

Slavery in America and in the Roman Empire
アメリカの奴隷とローマ帝国の奴隷

There is a saying in America, even among some Americans. They say that America began with two great crimes. Those are the extermination of the Indians, and the importation of Black slaves from Africa.

アメリカでは、一部のアメリカ人の間に、次のような格言があります。アメリカは、二つの大きな犯罪から始まった。それは、アメリカ・インディアンの根絶と、アフリカからの黒人奴隷の輸入である、というものです。

The Indians, well I will write about that at a later time. Let us discuss Black people, well I suppose the current term is African Americans. The names by which you can politely refer to people changes rapidly in modern America.

アメリカ・インディアンについては別の機会に書きたいと思いますが、ここでは、黒人の話をしましょう。まあ、現在の正しい言葉では、「アフリカ系アメリカ人」でしょう。現代のアメリカ人の会話では、こうした、人を丁寧に表す言葉が急速に広まりました。

First of all, I will explain what a slave was. Japanese people have a very dim conception of this. Japanese people have no experience of slavery.

100

第 4 章　アメリカの人種問題

　最初に、奴隷とはどのようなものであったのかを説明します。日本には奴隷制がなかったので、日本人の皆さんは、このことが少し分かりづらいかと思います。

What it means is that a person is not a person, but owned property. You cannot make any decisions about your life at all. Anything that you wear comes from the Master. Everything that you eat comes from the Master.

　奴隷という言葉が意味するものは、人が人ではなく、いわゆる主人（マスター）と呼ばれる他者に隷属し、彼らが所有する財産であるということです。自分の人生について、何も決定することができません。着る服もすべて主人が決め、食べものもすべて主人から与えられます。

If you have sexual relations with a woman, your children are the property of the Master. He can sell them at any time. He can kill them if he likes.

　例えば、あなたが奴隷だとしましょう。もしあなたがある女性とセックスをしたら、その子供は主人の財産であり、その主人の気持ちひとつで、いつでもその子供を売ることができます。殺したいと思えば、その子供を殺しても、何の問題もありません。

The woman who birthed your children, the Master has sexual privileges whenever he wishes. He can kill her if he wishes.

　また、あなたの子供を産んだ女性と主人は、好きな時にセックスをすることができます。主人がその女性を殺したいなら、殺すこともできます。

You have no existence.

　あなたは存在していません。

101

Chapter4 The problem of race in America

In Imperial Rome, there were slaves. But there were crucial differences between American and Imperial Roman slavery. In Imperial Rome, sometimes slaves were quite educated, and literate in several languages. Such slaves were respected by their owners, and treated well. They performed valuable work for their owners.

ローマ帝国にも奴隷がいました。しかし、ローマ帝国とアメリカの奴隷制には、大きな違いがあります。ローマ帝国の場合、奴隷によっては教育のレベルが高く、数カ国語を話すことができる奴隷も

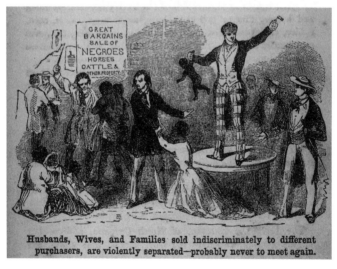

"Husbands, Wives, and Families sold indiscriminately to different purchasers, are violently separated --- probably never to meet again" "GREAT BARGAINS SALE OF NEGROES HORSES CATTLE & OTHER PROPERTY"

「家族は無理やり引き離されて別々の買い手に売られ、おそらく二度と会うことはない」という説明が付いたイラスト (1853年)。壁には「黒人、馬、牛、その他、大バーゲン」という貼り紙もある。

第4章　アメリカの人種問題

いました。そのような奴隷は主人から敬意を払われ、丁重な扱いを受け、主人のために価値ある仕事を任されました。

In Imperial Rome, racial prejudice based on skin color did not exist, not like in America.

そして、ローマ帝国では、皮膚の色による差別はありませんでした。これもアメリカとは違います。

In Imperial Rome, slaves often did attain their freedom. In America, it did happen that slaves did attain their freedom, but it was rare. In America, in states where slavery was legal, it was illegal for slaves to read.

ローマ帝国では、奴隷もしばしば自由を獲得することができました。アメリカでも、奴隷が自由を獲得することはありましたが、それは、ごくまれなケースでした。アメリカの場合、奴隷制度が合法の州では、奴隷が文字を読むことは非合法でした。

So unlike Imperial Rome, there were no slaves who were say, accountants, or record keepers or any such job. In fact, if it was found that a slave could read, he was killed. White Americans were afraid that an educated Black man might lead a slave revolt.

ローマ帝国と違って、会計士や記録係の仕事をする奴隷はアメリカにはおらず、もし、ある奴隷が文字を読めることが分かったら、その奴隷は殺されました。アメリカの白人たちは、教育された黒人が現れたら、反奴隷革命のリーダーになるのではないかと恐れていました。

And indeed, there were several slave revolts, all of which were eventually violently put down.

実際、いくつかの反奴隷革命の動きがありましたが、それらはすべて、暴力的に潰されました。

103

Chapter4 The problem of race in America

Black people were brought forcibly to America
アメリカに「強制連行」されてきた黒人

Slaves were brought from Africa in sailing ships, the voyage took about 6 weeks. They were packed below decks in chains, living on shelves. Between the shelves, there was not enough space to sit upright. On these shelves, they slept, ate, drank, and moved their bowels. They slept in filth, and were generally not allowed to clean themselves.

奴隷たちは6週間ぐらいかけて、アフリカからアメリカまで帆船で運ばれました。その船では、奴隷たちは甲板の下に並んだ棚の上に鎖で繋がれており、その棚の間で、まっすぐに座れるスペースがないほど、きつく詰め込まれていました。この棚の上で、寝て、食べて、水を飲んで、排泄しました。こうした汚物の中で寝かされ、自分の身体を洗うことも、ほとんどの場合は禁止でした。

About 15% of them died on the journey. They were treated worse than cattle.

こうした船で運ばれる途中で、15％くらいの人が死亡しました。それは、畜牛よりもひどい扱いでした。

From 1861 to 1865, America fought a Civil War. Many Americans will tell you that it was fought to free the slaves, but this is not true.

1861年から1865年まで、アメリカは内戦を戦いました。これが南北戦争です。多くのアメリカ人が、この戦争は奴隷解放の戦いであったと言います。しかし、それは、先にも述べたように、真実ではありません。

The South declared independence, The North attacked to destroy that independence. Freeing slaves was not an issue at the beginning of the war.

104

第4章　アメリカの人種問題

この戦争は、アメリカの南部が独立宣言をしたことに対し、北部がその宣言を認めず、こうした動きを潰すために攻撃をしたものです。戦争のきっかけに奴隷の解放は関係ありませんでした。

In the end, the war did result in President Lincoln declaring that all slaves would be free. From the end of the war to 1877, there was a period called reconstruction.

戦争は何年か続き、リンカーン大統領が奴隷解放宣言をし、やがて戦争は終結しました。終戦から 1877 年までは、復興と呼ばれている期間がありました。

This was to bring the southern states back into the Union. Also, it was to change the status of Black people from slaves to responsible free people.

これは、南部の州をアメリカ合衆国に再び引き戻すためのものでした。そして黒人を、奴隷から、責任を持った自由な人という地位に変える、という目的がありました。

But as I have written, Black slaves were uneducated, could not read. They came from many different tribes in Africa, and were only slowly developing a new culture. In 12 short years, it would be impossible to develop them into Americans like the White people were.

しかし、私が書いてきたように、黒人奴隷はそれまで教育を受けさせてもらえなかったので、文字を読むことができません。彼らの先祖はアフリカの異なる部族でしたし、こうした新しい文化を受け入れ、身につけるには、時間が必要でした。たった 12 年の復興期間では、新たなアメリカ人として白人のように順応することは、とても不可能でした。

And there was no effort made by the Northern states to educate them. They were simply put into political power by decree of the northern Armies.

105

Chapter4 The problem of race in America

　しかも、北部のアメリカ人たちは、黒人を教育するための努力は何もしませんでした。彼らはただ、北軍の制令により、政治的な権利を与えられたに過ぎません。

The result of this was deep resentment by Southern Whites, and the Ku Klux Klan was born.

　その結果として、南部の白人による深い憤りから、白人至上主義団体のＫＫＫ（クー・クラックス・クラン）が生まれました。

They practiced terror on the Black population in secret from US Federal authorities, and it worked. They were able to regain political control of the South, And Black people were prevented from voting.

　彼らはアメリカ連邦政府の当局から身を隠して、ひそかに黒人に対するテロ行為を行いました。それが成功して、白人が再び南部の政治権力を握り、黒人は選挙で投票することができなくなりました。

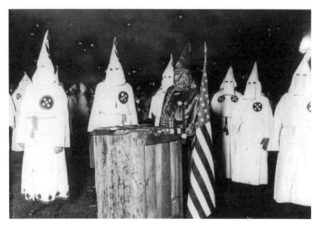

KKK (Ku Klux Klan)

ＫＫＫ（クー・クラックス・クラン）

第4章　アメリカの人種問題

During the years from the end of the Civil War to WWII, life was very hard for Black people. They were segregated into a separate society in every way. Southern Whites would say "Separate but equal", but the reality was that the resources committed to Black society was very small. The education at their schools was very poor.

　南北戦争が終わってから第二次世界大戦までの期間も、黒人の生活は、とても苦しいものでした。アメリカの中でも、完全に別々の社会として分離されていました。南部の白人たちは、「分離だが平等」と言っていましたが、黒人社会の方へ回された財源は非常に少なく、黒人の学校の教育は、白人の学校と比べ、非常に劣っていました。

There were many laws and customs that controlled them and kept them in inferior status. If a Black person was felt to have broken the law, and even thought to consider himself equal to a White person, he was often killed. A Black person who thought of himself as equal to Whites was called "Uppity".

　様々な法律と習慣によって、黒人は支配され、低い地位に抑え込まれていました。もし、ある黒人が、自分は白人と同等であるという考えを持っていた場合、彼は法律を破ったとみなされ、たいていの場合は殺されました。自分は白人と同等であると考える黒人は"Uppity"（生意気なやつ）と呼ばれました。

For such Black people, they would be kidnapped by a mob, taken to a tree, and hung until dead.

　このような考えを持った黒人は、暴徒たちによって誘拐され、大きな木のあるところへ連れていかれて、絞首刑にされました。

Reconstruction lasted only about 12 years. It was way too little, way too fast. Today, Americans fail miserably at rebuilding countries, they also failed in attempting to rebuild America after the Civil war of 1861 to 1865.

107

Chapter4 The problem of race in America

　南北戦争後の復興期間はわずか12年間。あまりにも短く、復興したと判断するには早すぎる期間でした。現在もアメリカ人は、いろいろな国の再建にあたり、同じような失敗ばかりしていますが、1861年から1865年にかけて行われた南北戦争の後の再建も、やはり大失敗だったのです。

The separation of Black and White society
分断される白人社会と黒人社会

Even in the North, there was segregation. It was not supported by law, but by custom. For example, Real Estate Agents would not sell homes to Black people, but pretend that there were no vacancies.

北部でも、同じような差別がありました。これらは法律ではなく、習慣としてです。例えば、不動産屋は黒人に家を売らず、空いている家があっても、空きがないというフリをしました。

The military was segregated into Black and White units until 1948. It was because of segregation that the famous Nisei Japanese American 442 regiment was a separate unit.

第4章　アメリカの人種問題

　アメリカ軍は1948年まで、黒人部隊と白人部隊を分けていました。こうして差別されたことで有名な、日系二世たちの第442連隊も、独立部隊でした。

During WWII, there was a massive movement north of Black people, they came to work in factories for the war industry.

　第二次世界大戦の間、多くの黒人が南部から、北部の大都市にある軍需工場へ働きに行きました。

But while they found social conditions in the northern cities to be somewhat better than the rural American South, racial prejudice was very strong among Northern Americans.

　社会的状況としては、北部は南部よりも良かったのですが、それでも、北部の大都市においても差別の感情は強いものでした。

There is a phrase called "White Flight". In this case, the word flight comes from the verb "to flee". What is means is, that when Black people began to move into neighborhoods in northern cities, White people

The 442nd regiment being reviewed by President Truman (1946)
第442連隊を閲兵するトルーマン大統領（1946年）

Chapter4 The problem of race in America

escaped into the suburbs. They did not mix. Only recently has there been a slight increase in marriage between White and Black people.

アメリカの英語で、"White Flight"（ホワイト・フライト）というフレーズがあります。この場合の、"flight"（飛ぶ）は "to flee"（逃げる）から来ています。このフレーズの意味は、アメリカ北部の大都市で、黒人が都心の一定地域に住み始めると、白人たちは郊外へ逃げるように引っ越しをする、ということです。白人と黒人は、親交を深めることはなかったのです。最近やっと、白人と黒人の結婚が少し増えてきていますが。

There is another phrase in the English language, "Last hired, first fired". The meaning is obvious. And it applies to Black people. After WWII, as Americans in general became middle class, so did some Black Americans. I think this was the best opportunity to have avoided the Race War that is now on the horizon.

アメリカの英語には、もう一つのフレーズがあります。"Last hired, first fired"（最後に雇われた者が、最初に解雇される）というフレーズです。この意味も明らかです。アメリカの場合、それは黒人のことです。第二次世界大戦後、ほとんどのアメリカ人が、中流階級になりました。黒人たちも同様に、だんだんと中流階級になりました。これは、現在のアメリカでまもなく起ころうとしている、白人と黒人の戦争を避けるための、最も良い機会でした。

But as the richest Americans have devastated the American middle class with the massive transfer of wealth that has occurred, Black people have suffered greatly.

しかし、アメリカの富裕層が富の配分を見直し、より強欲に利益を追求することでアメリカの中級クラスを潰してしまい、黒人たちは本当に苦しんでいます。

第 4 章　アメリカの人種問題

Today, Black neighborhoods in most American cities are centers of crime and hopelessness. There is a new word in America, "food desert". In a city it means that there is no store selling healthful foods within one mile. This is the Federal Government definition.

　現在のアメリカにおける大都市の黒人街は、犯罪と絶望の吹き溜まりです。アメリカでは "food desert"（食料砂漠）という新しい言葉が現れました。大都市で、1 マイル（約 1.6 キロ）以内に食料を販売している店がない場所、という意味です。これは、連邦政府が採用している定義です。

Over the years, America has tried many methods of solving the Racial divide. None of them have worked. One of the most difficult was concerning education.

　昔からアメリカ政府は、いろいろと民族の分断に関する問題解決を試みてきましたが、全部ダメでした。特に、教育については難しい問題でした。

I remember when busing started in America. In America, schools get textbooks and other infrastructure according to their local tax base. Since Black neighborhoods are basically poor, the schools have very poor infrastructure.

　私はアメリカで、すべての子供たちをバスで通学させるという計画が始まった時のことを覚えています。アメリカでは、各地域の税金によって、教科書や教育インフラを整えています。ですが、黒人街は基本的に貧しいので、学校のインフラのレベルも低いのです。

So the idea was to take children by school bus to better quality schools, which meant White schools. It failed. White people rioted. They set up private schools at their own expense. It was eventually given up.

　この計画は、スクールバスで黒人の子供たちをもっと良い学校、

111

Chapter4 The problem of race in America

つまり白人の子供たちが通う学校へ連れて行く、という意味でした。
でも失敗しました。白人が暴動を起こしたのです。白人は、自分た
ちのお金で私立の学校を作りました。結局、連邦政府はこの計画を
あきらめました。

There was Ebonics. This is the name given to the dialect of English that
many Black people naturally speak. So some people thought that Black
people should have school subjects thought in Ebonics instead of standard
American English.

もう一つの計画は、「エボニックス」、いわゆる黒人英語のことで
す。先ほども少し触れましたが、これは、数多くのアメリカ黒人が
話す方言のようなものです。そして、数人の教育者が、学校では、
黒人には普通の英語よりもエボニックスで勉強を教えるべきだと考
えたのです。

To get an idea of what Ebonics is, just listen to some rap music.

繰り返しますが、エボニックスがどのようなものかを知りたい場
合、アメリカのラップ・ミュージックを聞いてください。

But this was another great failure. The fact is, to succeed in America,
you must speak and read and write standard American English.

しかし、これも大失敗でした。現実問題として、アメリカで成功
するためには、スタンダードな英語を読み、書き、話すことができ
ないとダメだからです。

There is Affirmative Action. Basically, this was the concept of giving
Black people jobs even if they don't meet the qualifications. Of course, it
also means that some White people will lose out.

それから、"Affirmative Action"、積極的優遇（差別撤廃）措置と
いうものがありました。これは基本的に、基準に満たない場合でも、

第4章 アメリカの人種問題

黒人に仕事、特に連邦政府の仕事を与えるというものです。もちろん、基準を満たしている白人の何人かが、そのために仕事を失うことになります。

Among Black people, it has created a sense of dependent entitlement, and among White people resentment.

結局このような政策が、黒人には労働者としての権利意識を生み出し、白人には憤りを生み出しました。

Integration succeeds in the military
軍隊では、人種の統合が成功した

Americans keep saying that they will rebuild some country after they invade and destroy it. However if they cannot rebuild their own nation, from Civil War reconstruction until now, how can they rebuild a foreign country?

アメリカ人というのはいつも、どこかの国を侵略・崩壊させてから、それを再建するということをやっています。しかし、南北戦争の復興から現在に至るまで、自分の国ですら再建できていないのに、どのようにして他国の再建ができるというのでしょうか？

The one area where racial integration has succeeded is the military. Black people have risen to positions of command. They are obeyed by White subordinates.

アメリカ社会で人種統合が成功した一つの例、それは軍隊です。軍隊では、黒人が指揮をとる立場にまで上がりました。白人の部下が、その黒人の命令に従うのです。

113

Chapter4 The problem of race in America

When I was in Boot Camp, basic training, we were told that we were not White, Black, Brown, or Asian, we were all one color, Marine Corps Green.

私は海兵隊の新兵訓練所に入った時に、軍曹から、「私たちは白、黒、茶色、アジア人という、異なる色ではない。皆が一つの皮膚の色であり、それは海兵隊の緑である」と強く言われました。

I think it was due to the authoritarian nature of military society that integration could succeed there. Normal American society is very very anti authoritarian, and the government is weak.

やはり、軍隊の社会は権威主義的ですから、こうした人種統合が成功したのでしょう。一方、普通のアメリカ社会はとても反権威主義的で、政府も弱いです。

There is one subject that I avoid talking about when I am with Black friends. That is ancestry. Myself, on my father's side, I am a basically German aristocrat, but I am also part French and English aristocracy. On my mother's side, I am completely Swedish, but not of the aristocracy. And there are stories of a little Huron Indian ancestry.

でも、私にも、黒人の友達には話さない話題が一つあります。それは、先祖のことです。私は、父の方が、基本的にドイツ貴族ですが、フランスと英国の貴族の先祖もいます。母の方はスウェーデン人で、貴族ではない普通の農民です。それと、ヒューロン・インディアンの先祖がいるという話もあります。

I am proud of all of it. But Black Americans have only a slave background, unless their family came later from Africa. And in Western society, slaves are not human beings.

私は、こうした先祖すべてに誇りがあります。しかし、アメリカの黒人は、奴隷の時代の後にアフリカから来た人でなければ、ほぼ

114

みんな、奴隷の先祖しかいないわけです。西洋の社会では、奴隷は人間とは見なされません。

In an effort to connect with African culture, many Black Americans take African names. The famous boxer Muhammad Ali was born Cassius Clay, but he converted to Islam and took a Moslem name. The truth is, many of the areas in Africa just south of the Sahara desert, are populated by Black people, but are Moslem.

ルーツがアフリカの文化に繋がっているということで、数多くの黒人が、アフリカ的な名前を使います。有名なボクサー、モハメド・アリ氏は、本名をカシアス・クレイとして生まれ育ちましたが、イスラム教に改宗してイスラム名に変えました。アフリカ大陸には、サハラ砂漠から南の地域に多くの黒人が住んでいますが、多くはイスラム教です。

Holidays such as Kwanzaa, based on African traditions, have been created. It is celebrated in America from December 26th to January 1st, and emphasizes Black community, pride, cooperation. A Black American professor created this in an effort to help the Black community.

アフリカの伝統をベースにした、クワンザという祭日も作られています。それはアメリカでは 12 月 26 日から 1 月 1 日まで祝われ、黒人コミュニティの誇りと協力を強調しています。この祭日は、黒人教授の働きかけで作られました。

Black people who are too sensitive to prejudice
差別に対して敏感すぎる黒人たち

But today, I think Black people have become over sensitive to prejudice. Sometimes it seems they get angry over the slightest thing. Well, this is a

Chapter4 The problem of race in America

general American trait. All Americans are way too over sensitive these days.

しかし、現在のアメリカ黒人は、差別に対して敏感になりすぎではないでしょうか。彼らは、ちょっとしたこと、小さなことにも、すぐに怒りだすようになりました。まあ、これは一般的なアメリカ人の特徴であるとも言えます。現在のアメリカ人は、ほとんどの人が敏感になりすぎです。

Also, Black people seem to expect someone to help them. Well, this is due to government efforts to give Black people an advantage. The government efforts were never enough, or done in the right way, but it has left Black people with a sense of entitlement.

それから、黒人の人たちは、誰かが彼らを援助することが当たり前だと考えているようなフシもあります。これは連邦政府が、ことさら黒人に対して、社会的に有利な立場を与えようとしてきたせいです。連邦政府のやることは、いつも中途半端で何かが足りなかったり、正しい方法で行われていなかったりします。そのせいで、アメリカ黒人が権利意識を強く持つようになったのです。

Prejudice still exists in America. It is very deep, and will probably never be eradicated. Black people are going to have to overcome this. They are going to have to be better than White people.

差別は今もアメリカの中に存在します。それはとても根深く、おそらく消えることはないでしょう。黒人たちはこれからも、この問題に打ち勝つことが必要です。彼らは白人よりも努力をする必要があるでしょう。

This was done in sports. 100 years ago, virtually all sports were segregated. There were separate White and Black baseball leagues for example. Black athletes worked hard, penetrated White society in sports, and thrived.

第 4 章　アメリカの人種問題

　スポーツの世界を見ると、100 年前は、ほとんどの競技に差別が
ありました。例えば、野球にも白人と黒人で別々のリーグがあった
ように。でも、黒人のスポーツマンは一生懸命に頑張り、白人の世
界に入って成功するようになりました。

Now they are going to have to do the same in academia, business and
other fields. Yes, it is true that Black schools are poorly funded. But they
must work hard. They cannot create a separate society, or demand that
mainstream society change in their favor.

　これからは、学問、ビジネス、その他の分野でも、同じような努
力をしなければなりません。黒人たちの学校に、十分な資金が助成
されていないことは事実です。しかし、それでも頑張らなければな
りません。白人と分断された別の黒人社会を作ることはできません
し、自分たちに有利なように白人社会が変化することを要求するこ
ともできません。

They will have to work harder in the society that exists. The difficult
part is America is very quickly spiraling into Civil War. I just hope Black
people basically stay out of this.

　現在の社会においては、より懸命に、こうした努力をしなければな
りません。なぜなら、アメリカがだんだん内乱状態に入っているから
です。私は、黒人の人々がこの内乱に参加しないことを望んでいます。

If the White people of political Left and Right persuasions want to kill
each other, let them. Don't make it a multi sided war, with race as an
issue. The Black people will lose badly.

　もしアメリカの白人が、政治的な右派と左派でお互いに殺し合い
を始めたら、絶対に参加しないでください。そこに民族問題を持ち
込んで、内乱を複雑にするのはやめてください。それをすると、黒
人は大変苦しい立場に置かれます。

117

Chapter4 The problem of race in America

But in the summer of 2016, Black men began to ambush police officers. This has the look of the beginning of Civil War. It will not end well for either White or Black people.

しかし 2016 年の夏に、黒人の男性が警察官を待ち伏せして襲うという事件がありました。こうしたことが、内乱の引き金になるのです。これは、黒人にとっても白人にとっても、何も良いことがありません。

For several years, there have been incidents of groups of Black people randomly attacking White people in shopping malls and fast food restaurants.

数年前から、ショッピングセンターやファストフード店で、黒人のグループが白人をランダムに襲撃する事件が増えています。

And I have seen videos of demonstrators, lines of Black and White people hands together blocking an expressway. They are protesting police killing of Black people. White people in cars on the road speed up and run them down.

私は、高速道路で黒人と白人の抗議者たちが手をつないで、車の通行を止めているデモのビデオを見たことがあります。警察官が黒人を殺したことに対する抗議だということです。しかしそのビデオでは、車に乗っている白人がスピードを上げ、抗議者にぶつかって走り去っていきます。

The media avoids reporting on these incidents. I think the establishment controlling America wants to avoid race war. I now think it can no longer be avoided. It will go on until both Black and white people get tired of the killing and tragedy.

マスメディアはこのような事件を報道しません。やはり、アメリカを支配しているエスタブリッシュメント（支配階級）は、白人と黒人の戦争を避けたいと思っているのでしょう。でも、私の見る限

りでは、もう手遅れで、避けることは不可能だと思われます。黒人と白人の間での殺し合い、そうした悲劇に疲れ果てるまでは、終わらないでしょう。

The reality of a fragmented America

分断国家アメリカの現実

But prejudice in America is not limited to Black people. There is much religious prejudice among White people, of a religious and ethnic nature.

しかし、アメリカの差別問題は黒人差別だけではありません。白人どうしにもありますし、民族や宗教による差別も多いです。

More than 20 years ago, I spent 2 years in New York City. I had a friend who told me he was half Irish and half Italian. Right here Americans would laugh because they would understand the problems.

20年以上前のことですが、私は2年間ニューヨーク市に住んでいたことがあります。その時の友人で、自分はアイルランドとイタリアのハーフであると、私に教えてくれた人がいました。たいていのアメリカ人は、この話を聞くと、半分冗談で、「それは大変だったね！」と言うでしょう。その人の両親の結婚には、両方の家族から、さぞ反対が起こっただろうと分かるからです。

But Japanese people would think, "What problems? Are they not both White and Catholic?" But there are still problems. In the workplace, ethnic Italians and Irish might work well together, but marriage is difficult across any kind of religious and racial line.

日本人は、両方とも白人だし、宗教もカトリックだし、何が問題なのですか？と思うかもしれません。しかしそれでも、ここには問

119

Chapter4 The problem of race in America

題がたくさんあります。職場では、イタリア人とアイルランド人が仲良く仕事をするかもしれませんが、結婚は違います。宗教や人種の違いがあるだけで、困難なものになるのです。

Different Protestant groups might intermarry, but it becomes very difficult when we talk about Jewish or Catholic people. Despite what Americans say, inter mixing is very difficult and very slow.

キリスト教のプロテスタント派の中では、結婚はそれほど大変なことではありませんが、ユダヤ人、カトリックの人々の間では、非常に困難なものがあります。アメリカ人によるプロパガンダと違い、アメリカ社会の中で、様々なグループ間で結婚することは、とても時間がかかり、困難を伴うものなのです。

I have made a basic chart of American racial and religious rankings.

以下は、アメリカにおける、民族のランキングです。

"American racial rankings chart"

English, Scandinavian, German, Dutch
French, Italian
Polish, Irish,   Jewish
Spanish
Eastern Europe
Russian   Jewish
Chinese, Japanese
Arabs
Other Asians, South and Central Americans
American Black people   Jewish
African Black people
American Indians

第4章　アメリカの人種問題

「民族のランキング」

イギリス、スカンジナビア、ドイツ、オランダ
フランス、イタリア
ポーランド、アイルランド　　　　ユダヤ人
スペイン
東ヨーロッパ
ロシア　　　　　　　　　　　　　ユダヤ人
中国人、日本人
アラブ人
その他のアジア人、南米と中米
アメリカの黒人　　　　　　　　　ユダヤ人
アフリカの黒人
アメリカ・インディアン

I have listed Jewish people in 3 different places because it depends upon who you are talking to. Some people do not have deep hatred towards Jewish people, others do.

　なぜユダヤ人が3カ所に書いてあるのか、その理由は、アメリカでも様々な意見があるからです。ある人は、ユダヤ人に対して特に嫌悪する気持ちはありませんが、一方で、強い嫌悪の気持ちを持っている人も、たくさんいます。

But the general picture we see is a nation deeply divided, not at all unified like Americans like to claim.

　しかし、これを見ても分かるように、アメリカは、アメリカ人が主張しているような統一された国家ではなく、真実は、深く分断されている国家なのです。

121

Chapter5 Anti Trump and pro Trump forces

Chapter 5
Anti Trump and pro Trump forces
トランプ大統領に対する反対派と賛成派

Anti
反対派

The Antifa and the BAMN are two of the main anti Trump forces who have stood out so far. Here, I am not talking about some organization that organizes protests. These are very violent and secretive groups.

「反ファシズム運動（Antifa）」と「バーン（BAMN）」は、反トランプの中心的なグループです。私は彼らを、正当に抗議を行う組織であるとは思っていません。この二つのグループは、とても暴力的で秘密主義的です。

BAMN stands for By Any Means Necessary. They were founded in 1995. The meaning means to defend Left wing causes by any means necessary. Antifa started in Europe in the 1980's as an anti Fascist organization.

BAMN（バーン）は、"By Any Means Necessary" の略語であり、「どんな手を使ってでも」というような意味です。1995 年にアメリカで創設されました。Antifa は、反ファシズムのグループとして、1980 年代にヨーロッパで始まりました。

Both of them use violence to achieve their goals.

彼らは、自分たちの目標を達成するために暴力を利用します。

122

第5章　トランプ大統領に対する反対派と賛成派

You can spot them quite easily in riots. They wear black clothing, hoods, and black masks. In protests in Berkeley in February 2017, when conservative Milo Yiannopoulos was scheduled to speak at the University of California, about 1,500 persons made a protest outside the venue.

暴動のシーンを見ていると、彼らを簡単に見つけることができます。黒い服を着て黒いフードをかぶり、黒いマスクをつけています。2017年2月に、保守派のミロ・イアノポウロス氏がバークレーにあるカリフォルニア大学でスピーチをする時に、会場の外で1,500人くらいの人々が抗議を行いました。

Some 150 persons wearing masks and hoods arrived at the scene, attacking people violently. The riot then spread into the downtown, fires were set, and many businesses had their windows smashed.

The Twitter account of "Official Antifa" (https://twitter.com/officialantifa)
「Official Antifa」のツイッター・アカウント

123

Chapter5 Anti Trump and pro Trump forces

　そこに 150 人くらいの、マスクをつけてフードをかぶった連中がやって来て、人々に対して暴力的な攻撃を開始しました。やがて暴動が街の商店街に拡大していき、暴徒はあちこちに火をつけ、数多くの店の窓ガラスを壊しました。

These protestors identified themselves as BAMN. One of their leaders, a middle school teacher named Yvette Felarca, was interviewed on Fox television. When asked about the violence to businesses, she said that the businesses should have pressured the university to cancel the speaking event. So they were responsible for the event, and breaking their windows was justified.

　この抗議者たちは、自分たちがバーンであることを認めました。そのグループのリーダーの 1 人である、中学校の女性教師、イヴェッ

The Website of "BAMN" (http://www.bamn.com/)

「BAMN」のウェブサイト

第5章　トランプ大統領に対する反対派と賛成派

ト・フェラルカ氏は、フォックステレビのインタビューを受けました。そこで、商店街での暴力について質問をされると、彼女は、その商店街が大学に、その右派のスピーチをキャンセルするための圧力をかけなければならなかったのだと言いました。商店街はそのイベントに対する責任があるので、彼らの店の窓ガラスを壊すことは、正しい行動であったと答えたのです。

Yvette Felarca said that such conservative people cannot be allowed to speak.

このインタビューでイヴェット・フェラルカ氏は、そのような保守派の人間は発言を許されるべきではないと言い放ちました。

In April, one of the more organized militia groups, the Oath Keepers,

The Twitter account of "Oath Keepers" (https://twitter.com/oathkeepers)
「オース・キーパーズ」のツイッター・アカウント

Chapter5 Anti Trump and pro Trump forces

sent protestors into Berkeley, they came unarmed.

　その後4月に、民兵組織の中で最も組織的なグループの一つ、「オース・キーパーズ」が、バークレーに抗議者を送り出しましたが、彼らは武器を持っていませんでした。

A further speaking event on April 27 by conservative Ann Coulter was cancelled due to threats of violence.

　また、4月27日に行われる予定だった保守派のアン・コールター氏のスピーチは、暴力的な脅しにより中止になりました。

Yvette Felarca is a member of the Trotskyist Revolutionary Workers League, she and other leaders of this group recruit students from the schools where they teach. They encourage the students to leave their families, and live with them in a group. They are a cult.

　このイヴェット・フェラルカ氏は、トロツキズム革命労働者連盟のメンバーで、彼女と、その他のバーンのリーダーたちが教えている学校から、学生をスカウトしています。そこでは、学生たちに家族から離れて、グループと一緒に生活することを奨励しています。まるでカルト宗教です。

The mass media do not report Black crime
メディアが報道しない黒人犯罪

Black Lives Matter is a nationwide Rights for group for Black people. They started in protest against the shooting of Black people by police officers.

　「ブラック・ライヴズ・マター（黒人の命が大切だ）」は、全国的な黒人の権利主張団体です。彼らの活動は、警察官に黒人が射殺された事件に抗議をすることで始まりました。

第5章 トランプ大統領に対する反対派と賛成派

The problem is that most of the Black men killed were criminals. The Ferguson Missouri riots that occurred in 2014 were sparked by the shooting of Michael Brown, a Black man, by a White police officer.

ただ、問題なのは、警察官に射殺された黒人男性のほとんどが、犯罪者であることです。2014年にミズーリ州ファーガソン市で起きた暴動は、マイケル・ブラウンという黒人男性が白人警官に射殺された事件により、誘発されました。

But what the American mass media did not report was that Michael Brown had robbed a convenience store a few hours before.

しかし、撃たれたブラウン氏が射殺事件の数時間前にコンビニ強盗をしていたことは、マスメディアでは報道されませんでした。

The Twitter account of "Black Lives Matter" (https://twitter.com/blklivesmatter)
「ブラック・ライヴズ・マター」のツイッター・アカウント

Chapter5 Anti Trump and pro Trump forces

The thing is, being a police officer in America is a very dangerous job. It is like combat in a war, you can be killed anytime. In 2016 the killings of police officers reached a 10 year high. Some were deliberate ambushes, but most were random chance killings, where a Black person saw a chance to kill an officer and did so.

アメリカでは、警察官の仕事には危険が伴います。戦争における前線と同じで、いつでも殺される可能性があります。2016年に警察官が殺された件数は、過去10年間で最も多い数でした。いくつかは特定の人物を狙った待ち伏せによるものでしたが、ほとんどのケースは、ただ単に、黒人に警官を殺すチャンスがあったから殺しただけ、という事件でした。

The American mass media reporting is very skewed towards the Left, and does not report much of Black racial violence in America. It is not politically correct.

アメリカでは、マスメディアの報道はとても左寄りで、黒人たちの暴力事件を報道しません。なぜか。それがポリティカル・コレクトでないからです。

And many Black people are angry about the violence. 18% of Black people voted for Donald Trump. They have hope that he can do something to stop the violence.

しかし、多くの黒人は、そのような暴力に対して怒っています。黒人の18%はドナルド・トランプ氏に投票しました。彼らには、トランプ氏なら、そうした黒人による暴力を止められるだろう、という望みがあるのです。

These are people who are tired of continuous complaining by some Black Americans, and their continuous claiming of victim status.

このような黒人たちは、少数のアメリカ黒人による、永遠とも思

128

第5章　トランプ大統領に対する反対派と賛成派

えるような抗議と、永遠に被害者であるかのような主張に対して、うんざりしているのです。

The fact is, there is a lot of violent crime that occurs in Black neighborhoods, with Black people.　Yes, slavery was a horrible thing.　But it is taught in schools.　And it ended 150 years ago.

実際、アメリカの大都市にある黒人街では、黒人がたくさんの犯罪を起こしています。確かに奴隷制は残酷な制度でした。でもそれは、学校で教わることであり、150年も前に終わっているのです。

The destruction of monuments from the Civil War
南北戦争に関する記念碑の破壊

There is a group led by a Black professor in New Orleans, "Take 'em down NOLA".　NOLA means New Orleans Louisiana.　His name is Malcolm Suber, and he admits to being a Marxist Leninist.

先にも少し触れましたが、ルイジアナ州ニューオーリンズ市に、黒人教授がリーダーのグループ、「ニューオーリンズで白人優位のすべてのシンボルを下ろす」があります。グループのリーダーはマルコム・スーバー氏で、彼は自分がマルクス・レーニン主義者であることを認めています。

What they are doing is removing memorial statues of Confederate leaders, such as Robert E. Lee and Jefferson Davis.

前述の通り彼らは、南北戦争の南部の連合政府のリーダーたち、例えば、ロバート・E・リー将軍とジェファーソン・デイヴィス大統領の記念碑を破壊しています。

129

Chapter5 Anti Trump and pro Trump forces

Well, it is true that many American leaders were slaveholders, particularly in the South. This group states that they wish to replace the monuments with memorials to slavery.

確かに、アメリカの昔の、特に南部のリーダーたちの多くは、奴隷所有者でした。このグループの望みは、南北戦争の記念碑を奴隷制の記念碑に取り替えることです。

Well I see no problem with memorials to slavery, but I get angry about destroying those monuments that exist. Have them stand side by side. But today's Americans are not in a mood to compromise. They want their opinions and only their options expressed, other ideas must be destroyed.

奴隷制の記念碑を作ることには問題はないのですが、現在ある記念碑を破壊することに対して、私は怒っているのです。記念碑はそれぞれ隣りに作ってもいいでしょう。しかし、現在のアメリカ人には、こうした妥協の精神はありません。自分の意見だけを通したいと考え、その他の意見は潰さなければならないと考えるのです。

And this one thing, one of many things happening in America now, that could spark off a violent Civil War. On June 10th, 2017, many armed Right wing Texans gathered in a park in Houston Texas. They responded to an internet threat by Antifa that the Statue of Sam Houston would be removed.

このような過激な活動が影響して、一つの事件が、現在のアメリカにおける暴力的な内乱を誘発する可能性があります。2017年6月10日には、武器を所有している多くの右派のテキサス人が、テキサス州ヒューストン市に集まりました。ネット上で、反ファシズム運動（Antifa）によってサム・ヒューストン氏の記念碑が壊されるという噂があり、その反動として武器を所有している右派が集まって来たのです。

Sam Houston was one of the revolutionaries who was part of the war

第 5 章　トランプ大統領に対する反対派と賛成派

to take Texas from Mexico, a governor of the state of Texas, and a slave owner. Thusly the Marxist Left wants to destroy his monument.

　サム・ヒューストン氏は、米墨戦争において、メキシコからテキサスを獲得するための重要な役割を演じ、その後はテキサス州の知事となり、同時に奴隷所有者でもありました。こうした理由によって、マルクス主義の左派は彼の記念碑を破壊したいと考えたのです。

Texas is an "open carry" state, which means that guns can be openly carried. In response to this threat, many Right wingers, including militia members, came to protect the statue with their guns. The Left did not show up, so nothing happened.

　テキサス州は「オープン・キャリー」の州です。これは、銃を公然と持ち運ぶことが法律で認められているという意味です。このため、左派の脅しに対して、多くの右派が、民兵組織も含めて、銃を持って記念碑を守りに来たのです。しかし結局は左派が現れなかったので、何も事件が起こらずに済みました。

The Statue of Sam Houston
サム・ヒューストンの記念碑

131

Chapter5 Anti Trump and pro Trump forces

This destruction of history is classic Marxist technique.

このようにして歴史を潰すということは、古典的なマルクス主義
のやり方です。

But it is a matter of time before violence erupts.

しかし、実際に暴力の衝突が起こるのは、時間の問題でしょう。

There is too much hysteria about the American Civil War these days.
Early in 2017, a 70 year old middle school teacher in Folsom California,
Woody Hart, was forced to retire. The reason was that he showed a
Confederate flag in a class that was about the history of the American Civil
War.

アメリカの南北戦争をめぐっては、あまりにもヒステリックな状
態が続いています。例えば 2017 年の始め、カリフォルニア州フォ
ルサム市で、70 歳の中学校教師、ウッディ・ハート氏が強制的に
学校を退職させられました。理由は、南北戦争を教えるクラスで、
南部の国旗を壁に掲示したことでした。

On one side of the room, was the northern Union flag of that time. on
the other side, the Confederate flag. The school declared that to be an
unsafe environment for students, the teacher was forced to retire.

その教室の一方の壁に、北部の連邦政府の国旗があって、反対側
の壁に南部の連合政府の国旗がありました。学校側は、これは学生
にとって不安を与える環境であるとして、この教師を強制的に退職
させたのです。

There are so many things wrong with this. By saying that simply
seeing a Confederate flag will so traumatize children, we produce weak
individuals that will not be able to function in adult life.

第5章　トランプ大統領に対する反対派と賛成派

　このように、多くのことが間違っています。単に、アメリカの南北戦争における南部の国旗を見ただけで、子供の心に傷を与えると判断するような過保護な環境で育てたら、大人の社会では使いものにならない、弱い人間を作り出すだけです。

It produces temperamental selfish people like we see on the American Left today, who believe they should have total satisfaction, even if it destroys the livelihoods of others.

　こうした教育環境が、現在のアメリカ左派のような、感情的でワガママな人を作り出すのです。彼らは、他人の人生を壊してでも、自分は完璧な満足感を得なければならないと信じています。

The history of the American Civil War is extremely complex, and I doubt that I could get a job as a teacher in America. American Black people should quit demanding separatism, quit harping about the past.

　アメリカ南北戦争の歴史は本当に複雑です。私には、アメリカで

The Confederate flag

南北戦争における南部の国旗

133

Chapter5 Anti Trump and pro Trump forces

学校の教師の職に就くことは無理です。アメリカの黒人たちは、分離主義を求めることをやめ、過去に対する文句をやめるべきです。

Spoiled Black students
甘やかされる黒人学生たち

I saw one young Black woman protestor at Evergreen State college in Washington state on a video. They have a day where White students are forbidden on campus, to let Black people discuss racial issues.

私は、ワシントン州エバーグリーン州立大学の若い黒人女性が抗議活動をする様子を、ビデオで見ました。その大学では、白人の学生を学校内へ出入り禁止にする日があります。それは、黒人の学生が民族的な問題について議論ができるようにするためです。

One professor refused to go along with the idea. The students made a mass demonstration, demanding his removal. First of all, this is very strange. Why must there be a day without White students? I can understand a day to discuss racial issues, but all students should do it together.

これに対し、一人の教授がこの提案を拒否しました。すると学生たちは大規模なデモを起こして、その教授をクビにすることを要求しました。しかし、これは非常に奇妙なことです。なぜ、白人の学生がいない日を作らなければならないのでしょう？　民族問題を議論する日を作るということは理解できますが、それならば、すべての学生が、一緒に議論をしなければなりません。

The young Black woman I saw in the video was reading a manifesto to the school authorities. Yet she could not read about 20% of the words in the manifesto. Why is she a University student if she cannot read English?

第 5 章　トランプ大統領に対する反対派と賛成派

　私がビデオで見た若い黒人の女子学生が、学校の経営者たちに向かって声明文を読み上げました。しかし彼女は、声明文の単語の 2 割ぐらいを読むことができませんでした。この程度しか英語が読めないのに、どうして彼女は大学生でいられるのでしょうか？

I know several successful Black Americans in Japan.　They all speak Japanese.　You cannot succeed in Japan without it.

　私は、日本で成功した数人のアメリカ黒人を知っています。彼らは皆、日本語をしゃべれます。日本語ができないと、日本で成功することは不可能なのです。

So American Black people should stop worrying about Donald Trump, and learn English and other subjects to get ahead.　Yes, I realize that it is harder for a Black person.　So you must work harder.　No, it is not fair. But that is life, it is often unfair.

　ですから、アメリカの黒人も、トランプ大統領の心配ばかりするのはやめて、自分が成功をするために、英語やその他の科目をしっかりと学ぶべきです。黒人の人たちは、白人よりも一生懸命に努力する必要があるでしょう。これは、不公平なことかもしれません。しかし、人生とはそういうものです。時には不公平な時もあります。

The structure of the Deep State
ディープ・ステートの正体

Now I will talk about the Deep State.　This is the name for the establishment which controls America.　These people are corporate leaders, high military officers, top level bureaucrats.　Needless to say,　these people are secretive and difficult to identify.

135

Chapter5 Anti Trump and pro Trump forces

それではここで、あらためて「ディープ・ステート（Deep State）」について説明しましょう。これは、アメリカを支配している、支配階級という意味です。この人たちは、企業の社長であり、軍隊の将軍や高級官僚などです。もちろん、この人たちを、はっきり誰と誰であると特定することは困難です。

Since all major media are controlled by a few corporations, they can be considered part of the Deep State. America no longer has impartial news reporting, the news media simply spout the propaganda that the owners desire.

アメリカのすべてのマスメディアは、数少ない企業でコントロールされていますから、マスメディアもこのディープ・ステートの一部と考えて良いでしょう。アメリカのニュース報道は、もはや公平ではありません。マスメディアは、ただ親会社の望んだ意見を、プロパガンダのように繰り返しているだけです。

That is why the major media are so consistently against President Trump.

そのような理由で、アメリカのマスメディアは一貫して、反トランプ大統領なのです。

This entire story about President Trump and his advisors using Russia to influence the election is complete fabrication. It started in The Clinton camp to explain her electoral defeat. She did not want to admit she lost the election. So she blamed Russia.

ちなみに、トランプ大統領と彼のアドバイザーが、選挙に影響を与えるためにロシアを利用したというのは、完全に嘘です。クリントン陣営で、彼女の負けた要因を説明するために始まった作り話です。彼女は、自分の失敗で選挙に負けたということを認めたくないため、それでロシアのせいにしました。

Yet the media, obeying orders from their owners, simply keeps repeating the story as fact, even though no evidence has been produced. Even James Clapper, the under secretary for Intelligence, has admitted there was no evidence of Russian interference in the election.

しかし、メディアはオーナーの命令に従い、証拠がなくてもこの話を事実であるかのように、ずっと繰り返しています。国家情報長官のジェームズ・クラッパー氏でさえ、ロシアが選挙に干渉したことの証拠はないと認めています。

The mainstream media is not doing it's job of investigative journalism, but is merely repeating propaganda.

主なマスメディアは調査報道の仕事を行わず、ただただプロパガンダを繰り返しています。

And what can possibly be wrong with President Trump's desire to improve relations with Russia? That so many Americans are so against this, they must be insane.

それに、トランプ大統領がロシアとの関係を改善しようとすることは、何か間違っているでしょうか？　多くのアメリカ人がこれに反対していますが、頭がおかしくなってしまったのでしょうか。

Yet is these people who created the policies that have led to such a great wealth gap in America. They wished for Hillary Clinton to become President, and used massive cheating in the election to try to make her President.

しかし、こうした人たちの政策によって、アメリカの巨大な格差社会は作られました。彼らの望みはヒラリー・クリントン氏が大統領になることであり、それを実現するために、選挙で多くの不正を行いました。

This is because she is so corrupt and makes so much money from bribes and speaking fees, the Deep State people felt she would not make any problems for them.

なぜなら、彼女は賄賂や企業イベントの講演料をたくさんもらっていて、とても腐敗しているので、ディープ・ステートの人たちは、彼女なら何も問題を起こさないと思ったのでしょう。

What they did not count on was that the American people are armed and angry.

彼らが理解していなかったことは、アメリカ国民は武器を所有しており、しかも怒っているということです。

I am not sure how long President Trump can last. There is a very serious concentrated campaign to remove him. He does not really have the support of his own party. In the Primary election, the Republicans only reluctantly embraced him when it was clear that no one else could beat him, even despite cheating.

トランプ大統領がいつまで続けられるかは分かりません。彼を解任するための、集中的なキャンペーンも存在しますし、そもそも彼は自分の政党の支持をそんなに得ていません。共和党員は、予備選挙で、たとえ不正をしたとしても、他の候補者がトランプ氏に勝つことが不可能であると理解したため、しぶしぶ彼を認めたのです。

The meaning of supporting President Trump
トランプ大統領を支援する意味

Well I would like to ask the Deep State people a question. Yes, it is true that he is not a professional experienced politician. Well, frankly George Bush was in my opinion the worst President in American history. America and the world survived him.

第5章　トランプ大統領に対する反対派と賛成派

　ここで、ディープ・ステートの方々に質問をしたいと思います。
確かに、トランプ大統領はプロの政治家ではありません。正直に言
うと、私はジョージ・W・ブッシュ元大統領がアメリカの歴史上、
最悪の大統領だったと思いますが、それでも、彼のせいでアメリカ
と世界が崩壊することはありませんでした。

But to the Deep State people, is it so necessary to actually remove him?
Why not let him continue as President, and find a way to work with him?
If the government is truly controlled by various Deep State interests, this
should not be a problem.

　そこでディープ・ステートの人たちに聞くのですが、本当にトラ
ンプ大統領を解任する必要があるのでしょうか？　彼にそのまま大
統領を続けさせて、協力する方法を見つけてみたらどうでしょう。
もし政府が本当にディープ・ステートによって支配されているのな
らば、この程度のことは問題ないでしょう。

The thing is, the Deep State totally misread the Primary Republican
party elections. Preferred candidates like Marco Rubio or Jeb Bush could
just not compete with Donald Trump.

　問題は、ディープ・ステートが共和党の予備選挙を全然理解して
いなかったということです。彼らが好きな候補者、例えば、マルコ・
ルビオ氏とかジェブ・ブッシュ氏では、ドナルド・トランプ氏と競
うことはできませんでした。

There is a reason for this. The American people can no longer live.
They are angry. And they are armed. The militia movement has 100,000
members. They are all basically Trump supporters. That is enough to
overthrow the American government if they fight.

　これには理由があります。アメリカ国民はもう、現在の生活を維
持することができません。彼らは怒っていて、武器を持っています。

139

Chapter5 Anti Trump and pro Trump forces

民兵組織のメンバーは 10 万人です。基本的に、そのほとんどがト
ランプ支持者です。もし彼らが銃をとって戦った場合、アメリカ政
府を転覆させることができるのです。

Oh, a few leaders of militia groups could be arrested on some pretext.
But simply removing leaders never does solve people's war. New leaders
will arise. So what then, arrest every militia member as a preventive
measure? 100,000 people?

もちろん、数人のリーダーを、何か理由をつけて逮捕することはで
きるでしょう。しかし、単にリーダーを排除するだけで、人民戦争を
勝つことはできません。新しいリーダーは次々と出てきます。それで
は、各民兵組織のメンバーを全員、逮捕しますか？ 10 万人も？

Police and the FBI cannot do it. Only the Army could. And the Police,
FBI rank and file, and the Army have sympathy with the militia movement.
Many of them would join them in insurrection in such a case.

そのためには、まず警察と FBI では不可能です。そんな数多く
の人間の逮捕は、陸軍しかできません。しかも、警察や FBI の一
般的なランクの人、陸軍の下士官や一般兵は、民兵組織に共感する
気持ちを持っています。いざ革命となった場合、その人たちは組織
を脱走して民兵組織と一緒に戦うでしょう。

By destroying President Trump, the Deep State would be telling these
people who voted for him that there is no hope in America for them.
Remember, for them, he is hope. Actually, there is no way that President
Trump can bring back America's Golden age of the late 1970's.

ディープ・ステートがトランプ大統領を潰すことは、彼に投票し
た一般のアメリカ人に対して、アメリカではもう、あなたたちに将
来の望みはないのだということを伝えることになります。彼らに
とって、トランプ大統領は望みなのです。ただ実際には、トランプ

140

第5章　トランプ大統領に対する反対派と賛成派

大統領が、1970年代の、アメリカの豊かだった時代を取り戻すことは不可能です。

But a President Trump in place would buy some time.

しかし、このままトランプ大統領の時代が続けば、アメリカを救うための時間を作ることができます。

And with the Left, Political Correctness has become an uncontrollable monster, forcing sexual mores that conservative people cannot accept, destroying monuments to half of Americans who fought in the Civil War, violent groups like Antifa and BAMN who fight the Right wing demonstrators at every event. Feminists who wish to recreate the basic building block of society, the family, in their image.

左派について見れば、ポリティカル・コレクトネスは、制御できないモンスターになっています。保守的な人が受けいれられない性的な習慣を強制し、アメリカの南北戦争で戦った人たちの記念碑を潰し、反ファシズム（Antifa）やバーン（BAMN）のような暴力的なグループは、あらゆるイベントで右派の人と戦っています。フェミニストは、社会の基盤や家族制度を、自分たちの好きなように作り直そうとしています。

And the Right will not accept this.

右派はこのような活動を認めません。

If these people are not reigned in, by themselves they could provoke a bloody Civil War. But I think it is too late. Again, arresting a few leaders will not stop them. They feel that they have a right to complete satisfaction, no compromise with anyone.

このようなグループをしっかり制御しておかないと、彼らは血だらけの内乱を引き起こす可能性が高いです。でも、私はもう手遅れ

141

Chapter5 Anti Trump and pro Trump forces

だと思っています。もう一度言いますが、数名のリーダーを逮捕をすることでは、こうしたグループの動きは止まりません。彼らは完璧な満足を得る権利があると思っており、誰に対しても妥協をしないのです。

Now let us look at the pro President Trump forces.

それでは次に、トランプ大統領に賛成のグループを見てみましょう。

The militia
民兵組織

The militia. If you look up the word in a dictionary, usually the word militia means some sort of reserve military force under the command of a government. In America this is different. When I use the term militia for America, it means a volunteer force that is not under any government control. They are totally independent. In fact, most of them regard the Federal government as an enemy.

民兵組織。辞書でこの単語を調べると、だいたい "militia" という単語は、政府の支配を受けている国軍の予備兵であると書かれています。でも、アメリカでは違います。アメリカにおいて、英語で "militia"、日本語で「民兵組織」という場合は、政府に支配されていないボランティア部隊という意味になります。彼らは完全に独立した組織です。正直に言うと、このグループのほとんどのメンバーが、アメリカ政府を敵だと思っています。

They are almost exclusively rural and small town, politically Right wing, White, (although I have seen videos of a few Black members) conservative Christian, meaning something akin to Christian fundamentalism.

彼らは、ほとんどが地方の小さな町にいて、政治的には右派であ

142

第5章　トランプ大統領に対する反対派と賛成派

り、白人であり（ビデオで数人の黒人メンバーを見たことはありますが）、キリスト教原理主義に近い、保守的なキリスト教徒です。

Informed estimates put their numbers at about 100,000, in over 1,000 different groups nationwide. Many of them are former active duty military personnel, and have combat experience in Iraq, Afghanistan, or even Vietnam.

ある試算によれば、全国のメンバーの数は10万人、グループの数は1,000以上です。このメンバーの多くは元アメリカ兵で、イラクやアフガニスタン、ベトナム戦争などの戦場経験者が多いです。

Here we have a crucial difference with the Antifa and BAMN, because in a Civil War, combat experience will be very important.

そうした点で、これら民兵組織のメンバーと、反ファシズム運動（Antifa）やバーン（BAMN）のメンバーは、大きく異なっています。実際に内乱となった場合には、戦場での経験がとても重要になります。

Notable militia groups are The Oath Keepers, and the III%ers(The Three Percenters). The Oath Keepers, who claim 30,000 members, their name means they have made an oath to protect American freedoms guaranteed by the Constitution. The III%ers refers to that 3% of Americans fought in the Revolutionary Army in the American Revolution.

このような民兵組織のうち、注目に値するグループは、先に少し触れた「オース・キーパーズ（誓いの守護者）」と「III%ers（The Three Percenters）」です。「オース・キーパーズ」は、3万人のメンバーがいると主張しており、彼らの名前は、アメリカの憲法で約束された自由を守るという意味から来ています。一方の「III%ers」の意味は、アメリカの独立戦争で3%のアメリカ人が戦ったということを指しています。

So their numbers have greatly increased, particularly during the

143

Chapter5 Anti Trump and pro Trump forces

Presidency of Barack Obama.

オバマ政権の時に、特に、こうした団体の数が増えました。

There have always been such groups in American history, but in recent years their numbers have increased greatly. The Ruby ridge incident of 1992, where a former US soldier named Randy Weaver and his family were under siege by the Federal government over suspected firearms violations. The siege ended with several people killed.

アメリカの歴史の中には、いつもこのようなグループがいましたが、近年とくに、彼らの数が急速に増えています。1992 年のルビーリッジ事件では、元アメリカ兵ランディー・ウェイバー氏とその家族が、銃器犯罪の容疑で連邦政府に包囲され、その攻撃によって数人が殺されて終わりました。

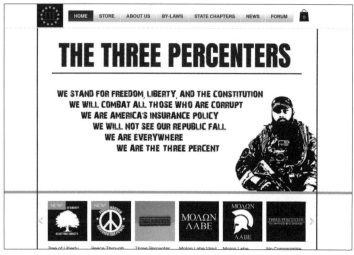

The Website of "III%ers" (https://www.thethreepercenters.org/)

「III%ers」のウェブサイト

第5章　トランプ大統領に対する反対派と賛成派

In 1993, a religious cult called the Branch Davidians was laid siege to for 51 days in Waco Texas in 1993. In the final assault, some 51 cult members died. The cause of the deaths are still difficult to know, but the FBI did take extreme care not to kill people. The compound burned down, and the members refused to leave, preferring death.

1993年には、テキサス州ウェーコ市で、「ブランチ・ダビディアン」と呼ばれるカルト教団への、51日間の包囲攻撃がありました。最後の攻撃では、カルト教団の51人のメンバーが死亡しました。死因はまだ不明ですが、FBIは彼らを殺さないように十分、注意を払いました。教団の建物が火に包まれましたが、メンバーたちはそこから脱出することを拒否して、そこで死ぬことを選んだのです。

These events have convinced many rural Americans that the federal government is trying to confiscate their guns, and impose a dictatorship upon America. You can find many sites on the net where paranoid people rant about UN Black Helicopters, that will bring in foreign troops to enslave Americans.

これらの事件によって、連邦政府は国民から銃を取り上げ、アメリカに独裁主義政権を作ろうとしていると、数多くの地方の人たちが確信を持つようになっています。その結果、ネットにも陰謀論があふれ、「国連の黒いヘリコプターが外国人兵士を連れてきて、アメリカ人を奴隷にする！」と偏執症の人がわめいているようなサイトがたくさんあります。

Some notable militia actions
注目に値する民兵組織の活動

The 1995 Oklahoma City bombing. On April 19th, 1995 Timothy Mc Veigh with one other person parked a truck outside the Federal office

145

Chapter5 Anti Trump and pro Trump forces

building in Oklahoma City, Oklahoma. Inside the truck was a homemade bomb, which detonated killing 168 people.

1995 年 4 月 19 日のオクラホマシティ爆破事件では、ティモシー・マクベイ氏と仲間が、オクラホマ州オクラホマシティの連邦政府ビルの外にトラックを駐車しました。トラックの中には手作りの爆弾があり、彼らはこれを爆発させて 168 人を殺しました。

Although it has not been proven that he was a member, he did have ties and sympathies to militia groups. He was executed for the crime.

彼がメンバーであるという証拠は見つかっていませんが、ある民兵組織のグループとつながりがあり、彼らの活動に共感を持っていました。彼は、その犯罪で死刑になりました。

The Bundy ranch. Cliven Bundy is a rancher in Nevada. He had a long time dispute over land ownership with the Federal Government. In 2014, he defied a court order to remove his cows from land the federal government claimed. 200 Federal Agents arrived to confiscate the cows. The militia movement responded, they claim 5,000 members arrived.

次はバンディー牧場事件です。クライブン・バンディー氏は、ネバダ州の牧場主です。長いあいだ連邦政府と、ある土地の所有権について争っていました。2014 年に、連邦政府が主張している土地からバンディー氏の牛を連れ出すようにという裁判所の命令を拒否すると、200 人の連邦政府の警察官が彼の牛を押収するためにやって来ました。これに対して、民兵組織が反対する動きをみせ、彼らの話では 5,000 人のメンバーが集まってきたということです。

Other sources put the number at 1,500 or less, but in any case they were armed with automatic rifles, while the Federal agents only had handguns. The Federal agents backed down and left, avoiding a firefight. The militia consider this a major victory.

第 5 章　トランプ大統領に対する反対派と賛成派

　他の情報源では、集まった民兵組織のメンバーの数は 1,500 人以下ということでしたが、それでも彼らは、自動小銃を持っていました。それに対し、連邦政府の警察官は拳銃しか持っていません。その結果、連邦政府側がその場から撤退して、銃撃戦は避けられました。民兵組織からすれば、これは大勝利です。

For some years, the militia have been conducting volunteer patrols of the American/Mexican border, to stop illegal immigrants from entering the US. While they carry automatic weapons, they do not shoot but call Border Patrol agents when they spot illegal aliens.

　何年にもわたって、民兵組織は、アメリカへの不法入国を阻止するために、アメリカ・メキシコ国境の巡回をボランティアで行っています。彼らは自動小銃を持っていますが、不法入国者を発見した際にも発砲はせず、国境警備隊に連絡しています。

Just before the election, both the Oath Keepers and the III%ers threatened to march on Washington D.C. if Hillary Clinton won. Since many of the militia members are former military, and the volunteer military in the US is basically a conservative Right wing organization, it is unlikely that military units would fire upon them.

　大統領選挙の直前、「オース・キーパーズ」と「III%ers」の両方のグループが、ヒラリー・クリントン氏が当選した場合には、ワシントン D.C. に進撃すると脅しました。民兵組織のメンバーには元軍人が多く、アメリカの志願軍の多くは保守・右派の組織ですから、彼らがワシントン D.C. に進撃したとしても、軍隊がこうした民兵組織を撃つことはないでしょう。

In fact, I believe it is likely that many rank and file members would join them in a crisis. This is because they are of the same background and economic class. The American militia represent a potential organized and capable guerrilla army in the United States.

Chapter5 Anti Trump and pro Trump forces

正直に言うと、私は、そのような危機の時には、数多くの一般兵士が民兵組織に合流するだろうと思っています。なぜなら、彼らの育ちや経済的なランクは、だいたい同じですから。アメリカの民兵組織は、アメリカ合衆国における潜在的、組織的、有能なゲリラ軍なのです。

The politically correct social policies promoted by the Left, such as Transgenderism, destroying monuments to Civil War heroes of the Southern side, irritate these people greatly.

アメリカの左派による、ポリティカル・コレクトネスを中心とした社会政策、例えばトランスジェンダー主義や、南北戦争における南軍の英雄の記念碑を破壊する活動などは、こうした民兵組織のメンバーたちをイラつかせます。

They are conservative, and they want to protect a conservative lifestyle. I call them Traditionalists. Conflict is extremely probable in America, and many will die.

彼らは保守派であり、その保守的な生活様式を守りたいと考えています。私は彼らのことを「伝統主義者」と呼びます。このように、アメリカでは内乱の可能性が高まっており、それによって数多くの人が死ぬことになるでしょう。

Christian Fundamentalism
キリスト教原理主義

Basically, a Christian Fundamentalist believes that the Bible is inerrant truth, the word of God. For example, they really do believe that the world was created in six days. Most mainline Protestants believe that the Bible was written by men who experienced visions from God, but who may have made some errors in their writings.

前にも説明した通り、基本的に、キリスト教原理主義者は、聖書は間違いのない真実であり、神からの言葉であると信じています。例えば、地球は本当に6日間で創造されたと信じています。一方、主流派のプロテスタント宗派では、神から啓示を受けた人間が聖書を書いたと信じられていますが、彼らの書いたことにも間違い、勘違いがあるかもしれないと考えています。

There have been three waves of Christian Fundamentalist religion in America, in colonial era America, before the Civil War, and now post Vietnam war. The different thing about present Christian Fundamentalism is that they desire political power in America.

アメリカにおいては、キリスト教原理主義の三つの波がありました。植民地時代のアメリカ、南北戦争の前、そしてベトナム戦争後の現在です。以前の波と現在のキリスト教原理主義の違いは、今の信者たちは政治的な支配を狙っているということです。

The Christian Fundamentalist believes that if all people held their true beliefs, there would be world peace. The core of their beliefs is expressed by the Seven Mountains theory.

キリスト教原理主義の信者は、世界の人々が彼らと同じ信念を持てば、世界が平和になると信じています。彼らの信念の中心は、7つの山の理論です。

Let us look at the Seven mountains theory. They believe that there are Seven Mountains that are the pillars of society. These are:

では、その7つの山の理論を見てみましょう。彼らは、この7つの山が社会の基礎となる柱であると考えます。その山は以下の通りです。

Chapter5 Anti Trump and pro Trump forces

Arts & Entertainment

芸術とエンターテインメント

Business

商売

Education

教育

Family

家族

Government

政府

Media

マスメディア

Religion

宗教

To their thinking, for peace, each of these mountains must be dominated by Christian Fundamentalists. So for example, the future world of America they imagine, all persons who own a media company, appear on television as announcers, or are reporters, must be Christian Fundamentalist. All school teachers, from primary school though university, should be Christian Fundamentalist.

彼らの考えでは、世界平和のために、その7つの山をキリスト教

第5章　トランプ大統領に対する反対派と賛成派

原理主義の信者で支配しなければなりません。例えば、彼らの想像するアメリカの将来では、マスメディアの経営者、テレビのアナウンサー、そしてレポーターに至るまで、キリスト教原理主義者でなければなりません。同様に、小学校から大学まで、すべての学校の先生も、キリスト教原理主義者でなければなりません。

The same for government. In their view, only believers in Christian Fundamentalism can be politicians, or have the right to vote. All corporate CEO's, military officers, must be Christian Fundamentalist.

政府も一緒です。彼らの考えでは、政治家や有権者になれるのは、キリスト教原理主義者だけです。すべての企業の社長、軍隊の士官も、キリスト教原理主義者しかなることができません。

By the way, according to their thinking, Catholics, Lutherans, Methodists and so forth are not Christians. Neither of course are Muslims, Buddhists, or Hindus, Or Jews. You can only become a Christian Fundamentalist by being reborn, that means baptized again, in their religion.

ちなみに、彼らの考えでは、カトリック、ルター派、メソジスト派は、キリスト教徒ではありません。もちろん、イスラム教、仏教、ヒンドゥー教、ユダヤ教は、宗教だと思っていません。彼らの教会でもう一度洗礼を受けて再び生まれ変われば、キリスト教原理主義者に改宗することができます。

They don't openly identify as Christian Fundamentalist, but many Baptists and Pentecostals are of this group. Some 25% of Americans are very deep believers in this doctrine, and another 25% hold some of their beliefs.

この人たちは、自分たちのことをキリスト教原理主義であるとは言いませんが、数多くのバプテスト派とペンテコステ派が、キリス

151

Chapter5 Anti Trump and pro Trump forces

ト教原理主義だと考えられます。この教義を深く信じている信者は
アメリカ人の25%くらい、その信念の一部を信じている人は25%
くらいだと言われています。

They tend to be rural, White, the same people who voted for Donald
Trump for President, and the same people who form the militias.

彼らは、だいたい田舎に住んでいて、白人で、大統領選挙でドナ
ルド・トランプ氏に投票した人であり、民兵組織のメンバーのほと
んどがそうです。

President Trump and the Christian Right
トランプ大統領とキリスト教右派

During the Presidential campaign in the summer of 2016, I saw a net
article with a photo. The photo showed candidate Donald Trump in a
"laying on of hands" prayer ceremony. This is where many people gather
around you and lay their hands upon you as they pray, in order to bring
you power. It is something that Christian Fundamentalist do among other
religions.

私は2016年夏の大統領選挙活動中に、ネットで、ある写真つき
の記事を見ました。写真では、ドナルド・トランプ候補者が "laying
on of hands"（按手）の儀式に出席したことを紹介していました。
この儀式では、多くの人があなたの周り集まって、あなたの体に手
をおいて、あなたに力を与えるために祈ります。キリスト教原理主
義者が、このようなことを行います。

When I saw that, and that he had such support among the American
Christian Right, I knew he would be President.

152

第5章　トランプ大統領に対する反対派と賛成派

　私はその写真を見て、アメリカのキリスト教右派からそのような支持があるのなら、彼が大統領になる、と確信しました。

In Donald Trump's cabinet, Mike Pence, Rick Perry, Betsy DeVos, Ben Carson, Rex Tillerson are, in my opinion, all Christian Fundamentalists. The Christian Fundamentalists have never had so much political power.

　ドナルド・トランプ大統領の内閣で、マイク・ペンス氏、リック・ペリー氏、ベッツィ・デヴォス氏は、私の見方では、キリスト教原理主義者です。キリスト教原理主義者が、このような強い政治的な権力を持ったことは初めてです。

In the coming conflict in America, I call it a Civil War, I see Christian Fundamentalism becoming a religious political force for the Right. With the militia, they have a disciplined and trained armed force.

　間もなく起こるであろうアメリカ国内の紛争を、私は「内乱」と呼びます。右派の中では、キリスト教原理主義が政治的な勢力になるでしょう。彼らは民兵組織という、規律があり、よく訓練された軍隊を持っています。

On the Left, there is the Deep State that is cooperating with the American Marxist Left. However, they have made a fatal error. The Antifa and BAMN can make trouble, but they cannot take over the country. They are simply spoiled children.

　一方の左派は、ディープ・ステートの人々がアメリカのマルクス主義者と協力しています。しかし彼らは、致命的な間違いをしています。反ファシズム（Antifa）やバーン（BAMN）はトラブルを起こすことはできますが、アメリカ社会を支配することはできません。彼らは単に、甘やかされた子供たちです。

And the Feminists have no power or influence outside of major cities.

153

Chapter5 Anti Trump and pro Trump forces

　そしてフェミニストは、大都市の外では、何の力も影響力もありません。

In a conflict, it would be very easy for some few people to blockade an interstate expressway for example. Or to blow up some long distance high voltage power lines to cities. The big cities are vulnerable.

　例えば、内乱になれば、高速道路を封鎖することは簡単です。送電線を爆破することもできます。大都市は攻撃に対して非常に脆弱です。

I grew up in the American midwest. When I was young, people there would joke that Russia would do America a favor by dropping nuclear weapons on New York, Los Angeles and San Francisco. Why, because there are so many homosexuals there, for the true America, Chicago is important. The coastal cities are not needed. This is how people there feel.

　私はアメリカの中西部に育ちました。私が若いころに、ある人たちが、もしロシアがニューヨーク、ロサンゼルス、サンフランシスコという大都市に核兵器を落とせば、アメリカは助かる、という冗談を言っていました。なぜなら、そうした大都市にはゲイが多いからです。中西部の人たちにとって、本当のアメリカのためには、シカゴこそが大切であり、上記のような沿岸都市は必要ないのです。地方の人たちは、そのような気持ちを持っています。

At that time it was a joke. Now, those feelings are becoming real.

　こんな話も、昔は冗談でした。しかし現在では、かなり本気になってきています。

第5章 トランプ大統領に対する反対派と賛成派

The United States Armed forces

アメリカ軍

If civil conflict comes to the United States, the stance of the US military will be decisive.

アメリカで内戦になれば、アメリカ軍の立場は決定的になります。

Political Correctness has left the American Armed forces in deep disarray. Troops are promoted on a quota system so that minorities and women rise to the top quickly, while qualified White men are passed over. Under the Obama administration, the forced acceptance of Trans gender people and women in combat roles has been particularly severe.

ポリティカル・コレクトネスによって、アメリカ軍は深刻な混乱状態にあります。昇進が割り当て制度で行われているため、少数派のマイノリティと女性は急速に階級が上がり、資質のある白人男性がなかなか昇進できません。オバマ政権は、強制的にトランスジェンダーの人々を入隊させ、女性を戦闘部隊に加入させることを認めたため、軍隊内部は非常に厳しい状況となっています。

People of quality are often fired because of a remark deemed sexist. Many other qualified people are quitting in disgust.

能力のある軍人が、性差別主義者とみなされるような発言をして解任されたり、あきれて辞めてしまったりしています。

Let us look more deeply into women in combat and the Trans gender problem. The Obama administration that ruled that women could serve in combat roles, and that Trans gender people can openly serve in the military.

トランスジェンダーの人々や、女性が戦闘部隊に入った場合の問

155

Chapter5 Anti Trump and pro Trump forces

題を、もっと深く見てみましょう。先ほども述べたように、オバマ政権の決定によって、女性が戦闘部隊に入ることと、トランスジェンダーの人が軍隊でオープンに仕事をすることができるようになりました。

The world the Feminists want to create first in America, and then across the globe, is one of sameness. Everyone is exactly the same, no one has any differences. To their thinking, this will bring world peace.

フェミニストが、まずはアメリカで作り出したいと思っていた世界、そして次に世界中でも作り出したいと思っていた世界は、「皆が同一の世界」です。それは、誰もが完璧に同じで、違いのない世界です。彼らの考えでは、これによって世界に平和が訪れると思っています。

Thus the argument that there is no difference between men and women.

その延長線上で、男性と女性の違いもない、という主張が出てきました。

War is for men. It is physically exhausting. It demands a toughness of your soul to kill an enemy. And this infuriates Feminists, so for years, the military has been their target for change.

しかし、戦争というのは男性に適したものです。肉体的に過酷ですし、敵を殺すためには冷徹な心も必要です。こうした事実にフェミニストは怒り、何年もの間、軍隊を、そうした価値観を変化させるためのターゲットにしています。

They have kept insisting that the physical differences between men and women are imaginary, that women can do just as well as men in combat.

彼らはいつも、男性と女性の肉体的な違いなど幻想であり、女性も戦場で男性と同じように戦闘する力があると主張します。

第5章　トランプ大統領に対する反対派と賛成派

The Army has caved into political pressure, and frankly, has lied. They created different physical standards for women. For example, women do push-ups on their knees, while men do them on their toes.

　陸軍も、こうした政治的な圧力に負けて、正直に言うと、嘘をついています。彼らは、女性のために別の肉体的な基準を作りました。例えば、腕立て伏せの場合なら、女性は膝をついて行い、男性は普通につま先から行います。

But when women fail at tasks, the Army and the Navy ignored this, and promote them anyway. In 1994, Lt. Kara Hultgreen, a US Naval aviator, was killed attempting to land her F-14 fighter plane on the carrier USS Abraham Lincoln.

　しかし、女性が任務に失敗した場合には、陸軍と海軍はこれを無視して、そのまま昇進させます。1994年に、アメリカ海軍の女性パイロットであるカラ・ハルトグリーン大尉は、空母エイブラハム・リンカーンにF-14戦闘機を着艦させようとして失敗し、亡くなりました。

Naval Aviation is a dangerous profession. Many pilots are killed in accidents. But further research into training program brings something up. She had four strikes. In the F-14 , it was three strikes and you were out of the program, not to fly F-14 fighter aircraft.

　海軍航空隊は危険な職業で、数多くのパイロットが事故で亡くなっています。しかし、彼女の訓練成績を見ると、おかしなことがありました。彼女は4ストライク（失敗）となっているのです。F-14のトレーニング・プログラムは、3ストライク（失敗）でそのパイロットはアウト、F-14戦闘機のパイロットにはなれません。

But because of political pressure from Feminists, the Navy was in a hurry to create a female fighter pilot. She died. Even the ejection seats

157

Chapter5 Anti Trump and pro Trump forces

of jet fighter aircraft have to be altered for women. Since their bones are lighter than men, the ejection seat rockets must be weakened, otherwise it will kill a female pilot.

しかし、フェミニストからの政治的な圧力によって、海軍は女性の戦闘機パイロットを作ることを急ぎました。その結果、彼女は死んだのです。軍用機にある非常脱出用の射出座席も、女性用に改修されています。男性に比べて女性の骨は軽いので、射出座席のロケットを弱くしなければ、女性のパイロットを殺してしまうからです。

Women in a tank crew cannot do all the jobs in a tank. One of the nastiest jobs is repairing the tank tread, which breaks often. It is simply too heavy to lift for a woman.

戦車の乗組員の女性兵士も、戦車での仕事のすべてをできるわけではありません。頻繁に壊れるタンク・トレッド（キャタピラ）を修理する仕事は、戦車部隊での厳しい仕事の一つです。しかし、たいていの女性は、それを持ち上げることができません。

Also in infantry units, carrying a mortar baseplate or machine gun ammunition is too heavy: only men can do that.

同様に、歩兵部隊における迫撃砲のモルタル・ベースプレート（底盤）、あるいは機関銃の弾薬を運ぶことも、たいていの女性には重すぎます。これらは男性にしかできません。

But American Feminists ignore these facts.

しかし、アメリカのフェミニストは、こうした事実を無視します。

The United States Marine Corps conducted a one year study on women in combat. All male platoons competed with mixed male and female platoons to complete various infantry tasks. In all tests, the all male units preformed much better than the mixed male/female units. And the women

158

suffered many more injuries than the man.

　米軍の海兵隊が、戦闘部隊に女性を入れることについて、1年間、研究をしました。全員が男性の小隊と男女共同の小隊とを、様々な歩兵の任務で競わせました。その結果、すべての任務で、全員が男性の小隊の方が、男女共同の小隊よりも機能的に優れていました。それと、女性兵士は男性兵士よりも、多くのケガ人を出しました。

The only army to put women in front line units in recent history has been the Israeli Army. Yet they discontinued the practice. It was found that mixed units of men and women did not fight as hard as all male units, and in difficult times tended to surrender quickly, to protect the women from harm.

　近年では、前線の戦闘部隊に女性を入れた軍隊は、イスラエル軍だけです。しかし、彼らもその方針をあきらめました。全員が男性の部隊と比較すると、男女共同の部隊は一生懸命に戦わず、厳しい状況になると、女性兵士を守るために、すぐに降伏をする傾向があったからです。

Political Correctness and the American military
アメリカ軍とポリティカル・コレクトネス

To promote politically correct thinking, there are endless hours of sensitivity training. This training covers issues like homosexuality, women in combat, rape culture, and White privilege. The concept of White privilege is now popular among social justice warriors, they say that American society is very biased against non White people. That is true in some respects. But the way the Left tires to change things, is even worse and brings about more injustice.

Chapter5 Anti Trump and pro Trump forces

　近年の軍隊においては、ポリティカル・コレクトネスの考え方を促進するための感受性トレーニングに、何時間もついやします。このトレーニングでは、同性愛者の扱い、戦闘部隊における女性兵士、レイプ文化、白人特権などの問題について、左派の哲学を教えます。先述した "Social justice warriors"（社会正義のために戦う戦士）たちは、アメリカの社会には白人以外の人に対するひどい差別があると言います。まあ、これは、わりと本当のことです。しかし、アメリカの左派がやろうとしている方法は、より社会を悪化させ、より多くの不公正を招くでしょう。

Rape culture is the concept that a male centric American culture promotes rape of women. At present, male US military members must be extremely careful about what words they speak, or how they even look at a women. If a woman military member feels offended, they can be charged with virtual rape, or intended rape.

　先にも触れましたが、「レイプ文化」とは、アメリカの男性中心の文化が、女性に対するレイプを促進するという意味です。現在では、アメリカ軍の男性たちは、使う言葉に要注意です。女性兵がある言葉で感情をそこなった場合、男性兵がバーチャル・レイプ、あるいはレイプをする意志があったと、告発される可能性があります。

Virtual rape means no physical contact but the woman involved is uncomfortable with the words or actions of a man. To the Feminist, this is the same as actual physical rape. The meaning of the word rape has been diminished.

　バーチャル・レイプとは、たとえ身体的な接触がなくても、男性の言葉や行動によって、それを受けた女性が非常に不快な気持ちになる、という意味です。フェミニストたちにとっては、これはすでにレイプと同じなのです。つまり、「レイプ」という言葉が拡大解釈されているのです。

第 5 章　トランプ大統領に対する反対派と賛成派

And this sensitivity training takes away time from combat training.

　しかも、こうした感受性トレーニングのおかげで、戦闘訓練の時間が少なくなっています。

Also, many military members have become quite angry about white privilege training. While racial prejudice exists in normal American society, the military has long been integrated. I know this from my own experience in 1974 to 1976.

　また、多くの軍人が「白人特権」に対して怒りを感じるようになってきました。先述したように、普通のアメリカ社会には民族差別がありましたが、軍隊では、以前から様々な人種がうまく溶け込んでいました。私は 1974 年から 1976 までの自分の軍隊経験で、これをよく知っています。

Race was not an issue in command or promotion. White Marines would obey orders from a superior, no matter what the sex or race of that superior might be. Period.

　指揮系統や昇進については、民族問題は関係ありませんでした。白人の海兵隊員たちも、上司がどんな民族・性別であれ、その命令には従う。ただ、それだけです。

Male ROTC recruits have been forced to walk in red high heels while in uniform. Male military members must also wear pregnancy sympathy suits. These are strap on vests that have large swollen breasts and a swollen belly to imitate the physical aspects of a pregnant woman.

　今、男性の ROTC（予備役将校訓練課程）の新兵たちは、軍服のまま赤いハイヒールを履いて歩くことを強制されています。また、男性の軍人も、妊婦体験スーツを着て、妊婦を体験する必要があります。これは、ベルトでつけるチョッキのようなもので、おなかと胸が妊娠中の女性と同じようにふくれています。フェミニストたち

161

Chapter5 Anti Trump and pro Trump forces

の考え方によれば、これで、男性が妊娠中の女性の生活を理解することができるということです。

To the political correct social justice warrior, this kind of thing is wonderful. But the truth is, it is humiliating. And that is the purpose of Feminism, to humiliate men in the military. If strong men quit the military, then the Feminists rejoice. Unfortunately, the truth is it takes strong men to fight and win wars, weak men will give up.

ポリティカル・コレクトネスで社会正義のために戦う戦士 (Social Justice Warrior) たちにとっては、このような訓練は、とても素晴らしいことです。しかし、本当のことを言えば、とても屈辱的です。それは、フェミニストたちの目的、つまり、軍隊の中にいる男性たちに恥をかかせるということです。もし、こうした屈辱に反発した屈強な男性兵士が軍隊を辞めてしまえば、フェミニストたちは喜びます。しかし残念ながら、戦争を戦い、勝つためには、強い心を持つ屈強な男が必要です。弱い男は、すぐに戦いをあきらめます。

The Trans gender policy in the military has already created many problems. I have read of regulations that tell military women, that if they are in the shower, and a naked male walks in, they are not to react negatively. This could insult a Trans gender person.

軍隊でのトランスジェンダーに対する方針も、すでに多くの問題を作り出しています。新しい軍の規則では、女性がシャワーに入っている時に、裸の男性が入ってきても、否定的な反応をすることは禁止です。なぜなら、トランスジェンダーの人に対して失礼にあたる可能性があるからです。

By pushing too much political correctness, America has created a military that is more concerned about social issues than military performance.

第5章　トランプ大統領に対する反対派と賛成派

　こうしたポリティカル・コレクトネスを推し進めすぎた結果、ア
メリカは、軍隊としての機能よりも社会問題を優先する軍隊を作り
上げてしまいました。

It is hard not to conclude that the Obama administration willfully
attempted to destroy the American military. After assuming office.
President Obama fired 197 military officers who did not agree with his
politically correct policies.

　これは、かつてのオバマ政権が、故意にアメリカ軍を崩壊させよ
うとした結果だと考えられます。彼が大統領になってから、自身の
ポリティカル・コレクトネスの方針に反対する軍の士官を 197 人
も解雇しました。

The continuing blunders of the US military
失態が続くアメリカ軍

What are some of the results of all this political correctness in the
military?

　このようなポリティカル・コレクトネスの強要によって、軍では
どのようなことが起こっているのでしょうか？

On October 12th, 2000, the destroyer USS Cole was anchored in Aden,
Yemen. It was attacked by a suicide boat. 17 sailors were killed and 39
wounded. When such an incident happens, the crew is trained to react
immediately, going to emergency stations to save the ship. But many of
the male members of the crew made the checking of the safety of their
female girl friends the first priority.

　2000 年 10 月 12 日、イエメンのアデン港に停泊していたアメリ

163

Chapter5 Anti Trump and pro Trump forces

カの駆逐艦コール号が、自爆艇によって攻撃されました。水兵たち
が 17 人死亡し、39 人が負傷しました。このような事件が発生した
場合、乗組員は直ちに対応し、緊急事態の場所へ急いで移動して、
自艦を沈没から守るよう訓練されています。しかしこの時、数多く
の男性の乗組員たちにとって、自分の「ガールフレンド」の安全確
認が第一でした。

Luckily, the crew was able to save the ship. But the Captain would not
be able to report the dereliction of duty, because it would reflect badly
on having a mixed male/female crew. Political Correctness has more
importance than military performance.

幸いなことに、駆逐艦は沈没をまぬがれました。しかし、艦長は
乗組員たちの職務怠慢を報告することができませんでした。なぜな
ら、軍艦に男女共同の乗組員がいることが、悪く見えてしまうから
です。ポリティカル・コレクトネスは、軍事よりも優先されるのです。

On April 7th 2017 on the orders of President Trump, 59 Tomahawk
cruise missiles were fired at an airbase in Syria. Out of 59 missiles fired,
only 23 reached the target. What happened to the other 36? Some sources
say Russian fighter aircraft, or anti air missiles. I have another theory,
American incompetence.

2017 年 4 月 7 日、トランプ大統領の命令で、59 本のトマホーク
巡航ミサイルがシリアの空軍基地へ向け発射されました。しかし、
発射された 59 本のミサイルのうち、23 本しか空軍基地には到達し
ませんでした。では、残りの 36 本はどうなったのでしょうか？
ある情報源は、ロシアの戦闘機や対空ミサイルによって撃ち落とさ
れた可能性があると言っています。私は別の見方をしています。つ
まり、アメリカ軍の無能力です。

Yet I remember US news reports at the time, they did not mention the
fact that the attack was a failure with 36 missiles lost, but rather that one

of the ships's captains was a woman. For me that is not important. What is important is why 36 missiles did not reach their target.

私は、当時のニュースをよく覚えています。36本のミサイルを失って、攻撃が失敗したということを報道せず、ミサイル攻撃を行った2隻の艦のうち、1人の艦長が女性であったということを強調していました。私にとって、それは大切な情報ではありません。重要なのは、なぜ36本ものミサイルが目標まで到達しなかったのかということです。

The acute incompetence of the US military
アメリカ軍の深刻な無能化

On June 17, 2017, an American Aegis destroyer, the USS Fitzgerald, collided with a merchant ship southwest of Tokyo. 7 sailors were killed. This is obviously American military incompetence, and the Navy has admitted responsibility. An Aegis vessel has radars that can see into outer space. Their job is to protect an aircraft carrier from enemy attack. There are two centers that are always manned on a warship, the bridge, and the CIC, or Combat Information Center.

2017年6月17日、アメリカのイージス艦フィッツジェラルド号が、東京の南西で貨物船と衝突しました。この事故で水兵7人が死亡しました。これは明らかにアメリカ軍の無能力であり、アメリカ海軍も責任を認めました。イージス艦のレーダーは宇宙まで届き、その仕事は空母を攻撃から守ることです。軍艦では必ず、艦橋とCIC、二つの戦闘指揮所に乗組員が常駐しています。

Both are manned at all times, both are equipped with many kinds of radar and sonar. So how did the sailors not understand that they were on a collision course? In two centers? In very busy sea lanes where they

Chapter5 Anti Trump and pro Trump forces

should have been watchful?

　この二つの場所には乗組員が常駐し、多くのレーダーとソナーが装備されています。それなのに、なぜこの軍艦の乗組員は、艦が衝突コースに入っているということを理解できなかったのでしょうか？　二つの戦闘指揮所があるにもかかわらず？　しかもその海は、数多くの船が行き交う、普通よりも注意深く航行すべき海です。

I think the only answer can be incompetence. Promotion quotas based on race and gender rather than competence, this has caused many quality people to leave the US military. So then we have people in positions of responsibility who cannot do their jobs.

　この質問の答えも、ただの無能力でしょう。昇進のノルマは能力の優劣ではなく、民族や性別で決まり、それによって、数多くの質の高い人材が軍隊を辞めています。その結果、その立場の仕事を遂行する能力のない人が、責任ある立場についているのです。

In the case of the missile attack on Syria, the Tomahawk should be a reliable weapon. It should be very difficult for an aircraft or a anti missile system to take down. I could believe Russia would be able to down 10 of them. But not 36.

　シリアへのミサイル攻撃を例にとれば、トマホーク・ミサイルというのは、かなり信頼性の高い武器であり、本来なら戦闘機や対空ミサイルで撃ち落とすことは難しいでしょう。ロシアが 10 本くらいを落としたということなら、まだ信じられますが、さすがに 36 本は無理でしょう。

So what might have happened? These missiles depend on computer programming to tell them where to fly. They fly very low, close to the earth. Their programming must be constantly updated to include any new obstacles, like a building or power line, that might have been erected. This means competent people must continuously monitor satellite photos, and reprogram the missiles.

それでは、この時はどのようなことが起こったのでしょう？　まず、これらのミサイルを飛ばすには、コンピュータ・プログラムが重要です。そして、こうしたミサイルは、地面に近い低空を飛びます。そこには、新しい建物や、出来たばかりの送電線があるかもしれませんので、ミサイルのプログラムは、常に更新する必要があります。つまりそれは、有能な人間が継続的に衛星写真を監視して、プログラムを更新する必要があるということです。

Also they must be maintained well on a regular basis. One of the biggest pieces of evidence that my theory is correct is the absolute silence of the media and the Navy on the failure of those missiles. With all the hate mongering going on about Russia in the US today, if they really had some kind of super anti air defense system, people would be screaming about a Russian threat.

また、ミサイルは常に万全の整備が必要です。私の推論が正しいという最大の証拠は、このミサイルの失敗について米海軍が沈黙しているということです。現在、アメリカ社会の中には、ロシアに対する憎しみに満ちた人が数多くいますから、もしロシアに、本当にそうした高性能な防空システムがあるということになれば、アメリカ国内で「ロシアが危ない！」と叫ぶ人たちが、たくさん出て来るでしょう。

But promotion in the military is no longer based on competence, but minority status or gender. This has taken precedence over competence. Accidents happen, and people die.

しかし、今や軍隊の昇進は、能力が基準ではなく、マイノリティであるかどうかや、性別といったものの方が大切です。能力よりも、このようなことが優先されるのです。その結果、事故が起こり、人

167

Chapter5 Anti Trump and pro Trump forces

が死にます。

As far as the Naval collision accidents, it turns out that training in seamanship and navigation for new officers was suspended in 2003. This was a six month course that all officers would take as their first assignment.

海軍の衝突事故に関連した話でいえば、2003年から米海軍は、新しい海軍士官に対する船舶操縦と航海の訓練を中止しました。これは半年間のコースで、新しい士官は最初の任務として、この訓練を行っていました。

Instead, now they are given a DVD set, and expected to train themselves while at sea duty.

それが現在では、新しい士官にはＤＶＤセットが与えられ、海上勤務を行いながら自分で訓練するように言われています。

Also, of women aboard Navy ships, 16% become pregnant and must be transferred to a shore station. That means somebody else must cover for their job. In the case of a person like a radar operator, this can be very important. It means the remaining crew members get less sleep and break time, become tired, and make mistakes.

海軍の軍艦に乗っている女性乗組員のうち、16％が妊婦になり、陸上の軍事施設に移動しなければならなくなると言われています。これは、誰か別の乗組員がその水兵の仕事をカバーする必要があるということを意味します。これが例えば、レーダー操作員などの場合には、非常に重要な問題となります。仕事をカバーする乗組員の休憩時間や睡眠時間が減って疲労が蓄積することで、失敗を犯してしまうからです。

And if America had to fight a war, say against any other competent military, they would lose badly.

168

第5章　トランプ大統領に対する反対派と賛成派

　もし、こうした状態のアメリカ軍が、他国の有能な軍隊と戦った場合、ひどく敗北することになるでしょう。

The weakened American military that Leftists want
左派が目指すアメリカ軍の弱体化

Standards exist in the military for a reason. I was a United States Marine. It is difficult to be a Marine, both mentally and physically. Marines are expected to go into the most difficult military situations and win, no matter what. And many of them die while doing it.

　軍隊の中に基準が存在するのには、それなりの理由があります。私はアメリカ軍の海兵隊に所属していました。海兵隊になるのは、精神的にも、肉体的にも難しいことです。海兵隊は、最も困難な戦場へ行って、何があっても勝つことが当たり前となっています。そのような戦いの中で、これまで数多くの海兵隊員が死んでいます。

I am very proud that I was in the Marine Corps. Yet the philosophy of Political Correctness say that such tough military standards are discriminatory. They say that every person should have the chance to be a Marine. If they cannot make the tests, the tests should be changed.

　私は、海兵隊だったことに、とても誇りを持っています。ポリティカル・コレクトネスの哲学では、そうした厳しい軍隊の基準ですら、差別的なものであると考えられています。彼らは、海兵隊に誰でもなれる可能性がないのであれば、それは差別であると言っています。つまり、テストに合格できない場合は、そのテストの基準を変えるべきだと考えるのです。

But then you no longer have a Marine Corps, you have a useless group of people. A major platform of Political Correctness is that for people who

169

Chapter5 Anti Trump and pro Trump forces

cannot handle, difficulty, insult, or other problems, remove the problem. In a controlled environment, like a university, that can be done.

しかし、それではもはや海兵隊ではなく、無用な人の集団にしかなりません。ポリティカル・コレクトネスの大切なポイントは、様々な困難や問題をかかえる人々のために、その問題をなくしてあげるということです。それは、コントロールされている環境、例えば、大学のような所であれば、このようなことができるでしょう。

But the nature of war is that people will try to kill you. You cannot say that you are stressed out, or insulted, or some other problem. You will then fail, and be responsible for the deaths of many of your countrymen, or perhaps the loss of the war and the nation itself.

しかし、戦争という場では、敵はあなたを殺そうとします。ストレスがありすぎるとか、屈辱的なことをされたとか、何か他の問題があるということでは務まらないのです。それで失敗すれば、自分の国の多くの国民が死ぬことになります。あるいは戦争に負け、国そのものを失うことになります。

But that is the type of military that American leftists wish to create.

しかし逆に、アメリカの左派が作りたいのは、そのような軍隊です。

Political Correctness is destroying the US military, and America's ability to police the world.

ポリティカル・コレクトネスは、アメリカ軍を崩壊させ、アメリカが世界の警察として活動する能力を奪い去ろうとしています。

Chapter 6

Where America is headed, and what Japan should do
アメリカの今後と日本の進むべき道

The unavoidable collision between Right and Left
避けられない右派と左派の衝突

On August 12th 2017, Right wing protestors marched in Charlottesville Virginia, to protest a proposal to take a statue of General Robert E. Lee from the American Civil War. They had a permit to march, from the city government. It was met by violence from Antifa and the Socialist Workers Party. Apparently, the police were ordered to leave the scene.

2017 年 8 月 12 日、バージニア州シャーロッツビル市で、アメリカ南北戦争の英雄ロバート・E・リー将軍の記念碑を破壊するという提案に対し、右派が抗議する行進を行いました。それは市政府の許可を受けたものでしたが、その行進は、社会主義労働者党と反ファシズム（Antifa）から暴力的な攻撃をうけました。警察は、その場から撤退するよう命令を受けたようです。

One person was killed and many injured. This set off a flurry of other violence across the country against monuments, and media attacks on the president. Why attack the president? Because President Trump said both sides were wrong.

この暴行により、一人が殺されて、多くの人が負傷しました。この事件は、記念碑をめぐる国内での他の暴力行為に発展し、マスメディアは、なぜかトランプ大統領への攻撃を開始しました。なぜマ

171

Chapter6 Where America is headed, and what Japan should do

スメディアは、大統領にこのような攻撃をしたのでしょう？ それは、彼がスピーチで、右派と左派、両方が悪いと言ったからです。

What the media don't know, or have forgotten, is that the election of President Trump avoided Civil War in November 2016. I was in high school during the Vietnam war protests. We had great internal discord back then that some feared might lead to Civil War. There was a phrase back then: "I may not agree with what you say, but I will fight to the death for your right to say it". Saying that, often brought to a stop many heated arguments between pro war/anti war, Right/Left people.

マスメディアの知らないこと、それとも忘れてしまったことは、2016年11月の大統領選挙で、アメリカは内乱を避けたということです。ベトナム反戦運動の時、私は高校生でした。当時、アメリカ国内は大混乱の状態でしたし、何人もの評論家が内乱になることを心配していました。当時、あるフレーズがありました。「あなたの

The statue of General Robert E. Lee
ロバート・E・リー将軍の記念碑

第6章　アメリカの今後と日本の進むべき道

意見には同意しないけれど、あなたがその意見を言う権利のために、私は死ぬまで戦います」。そのフレーズで数多くの、戦争反対・戦争賛成、右派・左派の激しい議論を止めることができました。

Then Civil War was avoided by withdrawing from Vietnam and abolishing the draft. But now there is no such magical solution, or such a magical phrase like there was then.

その後アメリカは、ベトナム戦争から撤退し、徴兵制の廃止によって内乱を避けることができました。しかし現在は、そうした魔法のような解決策も、あるいは魔法のようなフレーズもありません。

I think this event at Charlottesville has taken America from a low level insurgency to medium level. I say this because it has inspired spill over events. A week after the Charlottesville mess, a Confederate memorial statue was pulled down in nearby Durham North Carolina. The perpetrators are Communist party members.

私は、このシャーロッツビル市の事件は、国内の混乱レベルを、低レベルから中レベルにまで引き上げたと思います。なぜなら、その後、この事件と似たような事件が頻発しているからです。シャーロッツビル市の事件の1週間後には、近くのノースカロライナ州ダーラム市で南北戦争の南軍の記念碑が破壊されましたが、この事件の犯人は共産党員でした。

And I do not see any way to reduce the conflict. A high level insurgency would be when people start fighting with guns and terror bombings.

そして私には、こうした国内の混乱レベルを下げる方法が見つけられません。私の言う、高レベルの国内混乱とは、両サイドが銃で戦い、爆弾テロを行う時です。

I don't think even martial law would work now. Let us say that President Trump declared a national emergency, and ordered that all Antifa

Chapter6 Where America is headed, and what Japan should do

and Black Lives Matter members be arrested. And yes, Black Lives Matter has been showing a definite Communistic orientation. Since these organizations promote violence, I think the President has grounds to so.

たとえこれから戒厳令を敷いたとしても、アメリカは助からないと思います。例えば、トランプ大統領が国家の非常事態を宣言して、「反ファシズム（Antifa）」と「ブラック・ライヴズ・マター」のメンバーの逮捕を命令したとしましょう（最近、この「ブラック・ライヴズ・マター」という運動は、本格的な共産主義の形を見せています）。このどちらの組織も暴力を奨励していますから、私は、大統領がそのような宣言をするべきだと思っています。

This operation would be impossible. The media would criticize the President relentlessly. The feminists and the Democratic Party would also heavily criticize the President.

しかし、この作戦はおそらく不可能でしょう。マスメディアは厳しくトランプ大統領を批判し、フェミニストと民主党も厳しく大統領を批判するでしょう。

The President would have to arrest them all too. People would be killed. There is too much hatred, particularly on the Left, to craft any kind of political solution. The violence of the Antifa is increasing, it has become impossible to hold a Right wing political rally in America. The Antifa is guaranteed to disrupt any Right wing meeting.

結局、大統領は、それらの人々もすべて逮捕することが必要になります。その過程で何人もの人が殺されるでしょう。現在のアメリカでは、特に左派において、あまりにも憎悪が増大してしまい、もはや政治的な解決はできない状態です。反ファシズム運動の暴力は増え、アメリカで右派の政治集会を開くことは、もう不可能になっています。反ファシズム運動の連中は、どんな右派の集会でも絶対に粉砕すると宣言しています。

第6章　アメリカの今後と日本の進むべき道

American education tilts to the Left

ますます左傾化する教育現場

American universities have become centers of sedition. They are actively teaching destruction of the American nation. Many professors are giving their students good grades for participating in Left wing demonstrations. They actively encourage such participation. Some 80% to 90% of professors in America can be considered Leftists.

アメリカの大学は、こうした反政府的な扇動の中心になっています。彼らはそこで、アメリカ国家を崩壊させるための方法を教えているのです。多くの教授が、生徒が左派のデモに参加すると、良い成績を与えます。そのような活動を、強く奨励しているのです。アメリカの大学の教授は、8割〜9割が左派だと言われています。

Some examples.

以下は、いくつかの事例です。

A California professor at Diablo Valley College, also a lecturer in the State University system, Eric Clanton, has been arrested for attacking people with a bicycle lock chain during riots in Berkeley California in April of 2017. He is a member of Antifa.

カリフォルニア州ディアブロ・バレー大学の、エリック・クラントン教授は、2017年4月のバークレー暴動で、U字型の自転車ロックで人に対して攻撃をして、逮捕されています。彼は反ファシズム運動（Antifa）のメンバーです。

A professor at John Jay College in New York City, Mike Isaacson, writes about joyfully about killing his students in a future revolution on

175

Chapter6 Where America is headed, and what Japan should do

twitter. His students are future police and law enforcement personnel. John Jay College is part of the City University of New York, and has a good reputation in teaching criminal Justice and forensic science. He is a member of Antifa.

また、ニューヨーク市ジョン・ジェイ・カレッジの刑事司法学部の、マイケル・アイザックソン教授は、ツイッターで、将来の革命で自分の教え子たちを殺すことについて、嬉しそうに書いています。彼の教え子は、将来の警察官と法執行機関の職員です。このニューヨーク市のジョン・ジェイ・カレッジはニューヨーク市立大学の一部で、刑事司法と法医学の分野で高い評価があります。彼もまた、反ファシズム運動のメンバーです。

A professor of paralegal studies at Austin Community College in Texas, Robert Ranco, has resigned after tweeting that Betsy DeVos should be sexually assaulted. Betsy DeVos is the secretary for education.

ロバート・ランコ教授は、テキサス州のオースティン・コミュニティ・カレッジで弁護士補助員に関する学問を教えていましたが、ツイッターに「教育長官のベッツィ・デヴォスは性的暴行を受けた方がいい」と書いて、辞任しました。

A law professor at the University of Pennsylvania, Amy Wax, has published a document that Americans should return to traditional values, which she calls Bourgeois values. These include honesty, fidelity, thrift, temperance, punctuality, fortitude, gratitude, dedication, kindness, and loyalty.

一方、ペンシルベニア大学のエイミー・ワックス法学部教授は、アメリカ人は伝統的な価値観、ブルジョア的な価値観へ戻った方が良い、という論文を発表しました。その価値観とは、正直、忠実、倹約、節度、時間厳守、不屈の精神、感謝、献身、親切と忠誠です。

176

第6章　アメリカの今後と日本の進むべき道

More than half of the law faculty at the university signed a letter against her remarks, and the Lawyers Guild is trying to get her fired.

しかし、同じ大学の法学部の教職員の半分以上が、その論文に抗議する書簡にサインをし、弁護士組合は、その論文を書いた彼女が大学から解雇されるように働きかけています。

I think it can be said that America has never faced such crisis in education, where the majority of educators are dedicated to the destruction of the American nation, and actively promote violent revolution.

このような教育の危機、大多数の教育者が国の崩壊を望み、暴力的な革命を推進しているというような危機的な状況は、アメリカ始まって以来のことではないでしょうか。

Even in the teaching of hard sciences, such as physics or chemistry, the words used in teaching are being determined by political correctness.

例えば、物理学や化学のような自然科学の分野でも、教育に使われる用語をポリティカル・コレクトネスによって決めています。

Perhaps it will become necessary to close all American universities for an indefinite period, while such Left wing professors are purged. This is of course very un Democratic. But to do nothing is to simply let violent revolution occur, and many will be killed.

このような左派の教授を追放するためには、アメリカのすべての大学を、無期限に閉鎖する必要があるのかもしれません。もちろんこれは、民主主義的な提案ではありません。しかし、何もしないと、暴力的な革命が起こり、多くの人が死んでしまいます。

In a Democracy, the way to change society is by political campaign and elections. The present day Left wing is ignoring this, instigating violence to force their concept of change. This is very dangerous, not Democratic at all.

177

Chapter6 Where America is headed, and what Japan should do

民主主義において、社会を変化させるための方法は、政治的な活動と選挙です。しかし現在の左派は、こういった方法を無視して、自分たちだけの変化の概念を強制するために暴力を扇動しています。これは非常に危険で、全く民主主義的ではありません。

The State has the right to self defense. I am not at all against people of Leftist philosophy teaching in University. I am against people associated with or encouraging violent groups like Antifa and Black Lives Matter teaching in a University. Law enforcement should not be done by individuals, but by proper authority.

国家には自衛の権利があります。もちろん私は、大学で左派の教授が教えることに反対しているわけではありません。何に反対しているかというと、例えば反ファシズム運動（Antifa）や、ブラック・ライヴズ・マターのような暴力的なグループと関係し、奨励している教授が大学で教えることに対してです。法執行は、個人によって行われるべきではなく、適切に決められた職権者によって行われるべきです。

So what will likely happen? Basically, the two sides are urban Left against rural Right. And as a sub conflict, you have Black against White.

それでは、今後はどうなっていくのでしょうか？ 基本的には、「大都市の左派」対「地方の右派」、そして「白人」対「黒人」です。

It is obvious that there are many Deep State people and organizations out to destroy the Trump Presidency. But I don't think they understand the power of the Christian Right or the Right wing militia.

多くのディープ・ステートの人々、つまり、アメリカを陰で動かしている黒幕の組織がトランプ大統領を潰そうと画策しているのは明らかです。しかし、この黒幕たちは、キリスト教の右派と民兵組織の力を理解していません。

第6章　アメリカの今後と日本の進むべき道

Well, many of the American elite went to first rate universities, like Yale and Harvard. So they think they are superior, and know everything. They look down upon rural Americans as inferior beings. During the 2016 Presidential campaign Hillary Clinton expressed this opinion by calling Trump supporters "Deplorables".

まあ、アメリカのエリートというのは、だいたい一流の大学、例えばイェール大学、あるいはハーバード大学の出身です。彼らは自分が優れた人で、世の中のことはすべて分かると思っており、田舎に住む人たちを見下しています。2016年の選挙期間中、ヒラリー・クリントン氏は、トランプ支持者を「哀れなやつら」と呼び、こうしたエリートたちの気持ちを代弁しました。

The movement to demonize the Right
右派を悪者にしようとする動き

The Charlottesville event, well, there is more and more speculation on the net that is was an intentional set up to make the Right wing look bad.

ネットでは、リー将軍の記念碑をめぐるシャーロッツビル市の事件は、右派が悪く見えるように、意図的に仕組まれたものだという憶測が増えています。

I will write about it a little, since it changed so much. Some extreme Right wing groups had a permit to march in protest. They were protesting a decision to remove a statue of General Lee, of the Confederate Army.

私は、この事件によってアメリカが大きく変化してしまったと考えているので、もう少し説明しておきたいと思います。まず、いくつかの極右派の団体が、抗議のための行進を行うことに許可を得ていました。この抗議は、南北戦争の南軍の英雄、リー将軍の記念碑

Chapter6 Where America is headed, and what Japan should do

を破壊する決定に対する抗議です。

Many Left wing radicals, including Antifa, Black Lives Matter, the Socialist Workers Party and others came to confront the Right wing marchers. They came armed, some with baseball bats, some with automatic weapons. I have seen the photos of the weapons. The Oathkeepers militia was also present to keep the peace.

次に、多くの左派の急進的な人たち、反ファシズム運動、ブラック・ライヴズ・マター、社会主義労働者党とその他の左派グループが、右派の抗議者に対峙するために、そこへ来ました。彼らは武装しており、何人かは野球のバットを持ち、自動小銃を持っている者もいました。私は、その武器の写真を見たことがあります。そこには、平和を維持するためとして、オース・キーパーズの民兵組織も存在していました。

The police arranged the route of march so the Right wing protestors would go into a dead end street, surrounded by Left wing agitators. The Left wingers greatly outnumbered the Right wing. Then the police received an order to stand down, they left the area. They also ordered the Oathkeepers to leave.

警察が行進のルートを決め、右派の抗議者たちが行き止まりの道路に入るようにしました。これは、左派の扇動者たちが右派を取り囲むためのワナでした。左派は、右派の数を大幅に上回っていました。その後、警察は撤退命令を受け、そこを去りました。警察は、オース・キーパーズの民兵組織にも、そこから撤退するように命令を出しました。

The result was a massive riot. One person died when hit by a car. When President Trump said both Right and Left were to blame, the media attacked him. The media is worshipping the Left wing, yet they started the trouble.

180

その結果が、あの大暴動でした。一人の人が、車にひかれて死亡しました。トランプ大統領がスピーチで、右派・左派とも両方が悪いと言って、マスメディアから攻撃されました。マスメディアは左派を崇拝しており、そうしたことも背景となって、左派は暴力に訴えるということを始めました。

The media described the person hit by the car as deliberate murder, yet they did not mention that the car was attacked by the Antifa, they used baseball bats to smash the windows, it could well be the driver panicked and attempted to escape, hitting and wounding several people and killing one.

その、車にひかれて死亡した人に対し、マスメディアは、これは意図的な殺人事件であると書きました。しかしマスメディアは、その車は事件の前に反ファシズム運動の連中に攻撃されて、野球のバットで車の窓ガラスを打ち壊されており、それによってパニックになった運転手が、そこから逃げようとして集団にぶつかり、そのうちの数人がケガをして、一人が死亡することになったという、そのことに対しては無視をしています。

The runaway out of control Left
コントロールを失い暴走する左派

The whole event shows either incompetence or an attempt to create an event to destabilize the Trump Presidency. But I think the violence has now spilled out of control. The Left wing, the violent Antifa and Black Lives Matter, want Communist revolution.

この事件は、トランプ政権が無能力であると印象づけ、不安定な状態にさせるための試みだったのです。しかし私は、現在のアメリカは暴力がコントロールできない状態になっていると思います。左

Chapter6 Where America is headed, and what Japan should do

派、反ファシズム運動やブラック・ライヴズ・マターといった組織
は、共産主義革命を目論んでいるのです。

The Deep State is using these people to destroy the Trump
administration. This was a very bad decision. They have their own
agenda. Now, they are out of control.

ディープ・ステートはこの人たちを、トランプ政権を潰すために
利用しています。これは、とても愚かな作戦です。彼らには彼らの
目標があります。現在、彼らはすでにコントロールできない状態に
なっています。

The next week after Charlottesville the Right wing cancelled marches in
Boston because of so many Left wing agitators.

シャーロッツビル市の事件があった次の週に、ボストンで右派に
よる行進が計画されていましたが、数多くの左派の扇動者が参加す
ることが分かったため、右派はこの行進を中止しました。

People in Japan might think that all this protest is because President
Trump is incompetent. No. It is orchestrated by the establishment, the
Deep State, who cannot accept that Donald Trump won the election.

日本人も、このような問題の原因は、トランプ大統領が無能なせ
いだと思うかもしれません。しかし、それは違います。これは黒幕
たち、つまりディープ・ステートが行っていることなのです。彼ら
は今でも、トランプ氏が大統領になったことを受け入れられずに
怒っています。

So. From now on, civil unrest will continue. The Left wing is
increasing the amount of monuments to be destroyed. The Jefferson
memorial, Mount Rushmore, these are to Presidents who owned slaves.
So in the minds of the Left, they must be erased.

第6章　アメリカの今後と日本の進むべき道

　そして、市民の混乱は今後も続きます。左派が破壊を要求する記念碑の数は増え続けています。例えば、ワシントンD.C.のジェファーソン記念館や、4人の歴代大統領の顔が岩に刻まれたラシュモア山など、これらは、奴隷を所有していた大統領のためのものでした。ですから、左派の考えでは、すべてを消さなければならないのです。

The Jefferson memorial
ジェファーソン記念館

Mount Rushmore
ラシュモア山

There will be guerrilla attacks on these statues, it is already happening. The Right wing will respond. In the fall of 2017, violence will increase. Eventually, people will get shot.

　いずれ、これらの記念碑に対するゲリラ攻撃があるでしょう。すでにこうした事件が起きつつあり、それに右派が応じるため、2017年の秋以降は、さらに暴力的な衝突が増えるでしょう。そのうちには、銃で撃たれる人も出ます。

All this attacking history, and attacking White people in general, reminded me of the Cambodian Civil War that occurred during the 1970's.

Chapter6 Where America is headed, and what Japan should do

　このような、歴史を攻撃し、白人を攻撃する、ということから、私は 1970 年代のカンボジアの内戦を思い出します。

The Khmer Rouge, the Communist force, wanted to create a totally new country.　When they finally won in 1975 with capture of Phnom Penh, the city was ordered emptied, along with all other cities.　Anyone who had any kind of education was shot.　Anyone who wore glasses was shot. Anyone with any kind of technical skill was shot.

　カンボジアの共産軍、クメール・ルージュには、全く新しい国を作ろうとする計画がありました。1975 年にプノンペンを占領して、そうした都市に住んでいる人たちは全員、強制的に地方へ移動させられました。どのようなものであれ、教育を受けていた人は全員、撃ち殺されました。メガネをかけた人も全員、撃ち殺されました。何か技能を持っている人も全員、撃ち殺されました。

The idea was to create a totally new nation, composed only of farm peasants.　The Khmer Rouge said that time had now reverted to the year zero.　It of course failed miserably, and killed some 25% of the population.

　彼らの計画は、完璧に農民のみの新しい国を作り出すことでした。クメール・ルージュの宣言では、カンボジアの年代は 0 年になったと語られました。もちろん、彼らの計画は大失敗に終わり、人口の約 25％が死にました。

The American Left, with all it's redefining of racial roles, sexual roles and gender itself, and erasure of all history, seems to be going in this same direction as the Khmer Rouge.　It seems they want to totally erase present day America.

　アメリカの左派は、民族の立場、男女の役割、性別といったものを再定義して、歴史を消し去ろうとしています。つまり、カンボジアのクメール・ルージュと同じ方向に進んでいます。彼らはまるで、

第6章　アメリカの今後と日本の進むべき道

現在のアメリカを完璧に消したがっているように見えます。

Of course, America has many horrible things that it did do. All countries have some history that is not good. But the American Left has become insane in it's desire to destroy America.

もちろん、アメリカは昔、数多くのひどいことをしました。どんな国にも、良くない恐ろしい歴史はあります。しかし、アメリカの左派は、アメリカを崩壊させようとするあまり、狂い始めています。

The prospect of terror attacks by the Left
左派によるテロ攻撃の可能性

And as the Left increases it's craziness, the idea of a domestic terror attack cannot be discounted. Power lines, gas lines, these things make a city very vulnerable. A few people can do a lot of damage. I am not all advocating this.

左派がだんだんと狂気を高めるにつれ、国内でテロ攻撃をする可能性も高まります。先にも述べたように、送電線やガスなどのライフライン、これらへの攻撃に対して、大都市は非常に脆いです。たった数人で、大きな損害を与えることができます。もちろん私は、このような行為を推奨しているわけではありません。

And the possibility of someone attempting a cyber attack should scare anyone. And don't blame the Russians. If Russia wanted to destroy the US by Cyber attack, they would have done so by now. But they have no desire to do such a thing. They are a sane country.

また、サイバー攻撃の可能性では、誰もが脅威にさらされます。でも、それをロシアのせいにしないでください。もし、ロシアがア

185

Chapter6 Where America is headed, and what Japan should do

メリカをサイバー攻撃で崩壊させるつもりなら、とっくにそうして
いたでしょう。しかし、彼らはそのようなことを望んではいません。
ロシアは、まともな国です。

However, with the crazy self righteous young people in the US today,
they may feel justified in creating great mayhem with a computer. We are
already seeing this kind of thinking when the violent Left says, "Because
a Right wing speaker came to our city, we were justified in smashing
windows in downtown shops and lighting fires"

それよりも、現在のアメリカに暮らす独善的な狂気を持った若者
たちの方が危険です。彼らはコンピューターを使って誰かに大損害
を与える行為も正当なことだと考えるかもしれません。すでに、暴
力的な左派にはこういった考え方が出てきており、彼らはこう言っ
ています。「右派の評論家が私たちの街にスピーチをしに来たのだ
から、私たちが商店街の店の窓を打ち壊したり店に火をつけたりす
ることも、正当な行為である」と。

That is very scary thinking.

これはとても怖い考え方です。

The government is already planning for it.

でも、アメリカ政府もこうした攻撃の可能性を考え、その対応を
計画しています。

The government are doing game simulations of "Black Sky" events.
This is events like a major city losing electrical power for an extended
time. They say it is for natural disasters. But I think the real reason is to
find ways of dealing with loss of power and so forth to urban areas for an
extended period of time as a result of domestic terror attack.

政府は「ブラック・スカイ」事件のゲーム・シミュレーションを

第6章　アメリカの今後と日本の進むべき道

行っています。これは、例えば、長い時間どこかの大都市が停電に
なることを想定したシミュレーションです。政府はこれを、自然災
害のための準備だと言います。しかし私は、こうしたシミュレーショ
ンをする本当の理由は、国内のテロ攻撃によって大都市が長い時間
停電となった場合の準備であると思っています。

American urban areas will not fare well. The average super market only
has a three supply of food. People will riot. The country will descend into
chaos.

このようなことが起こった場合、アメリカの大都市は、すぐ混乱
に陥るでしょう。普通のスーパーマーケットには、３日分の食料し
かありません。街の人々は暴動を起こし、国は大混乱に陥ります。

I think, as I write these lines in August of 2017, the radical Left is
already too big for the FBI to control. And the military cannot do it. They
are incompetent. What do I mean by that? In 2017 we have seen some 4
collisions of US Naval warships with merchant vessels. In two of them,
some 17 sailors died.

私はこの文章を書きながら、すでに事態は手遅れであると思って
います。急進的な左派は大きくなりすぎて、もうFBIですら制御
することは不可能でしょう。軍隊にも無理です。なにしろ彼らは無
能力ですから。その証拠に、2017年、アメリカ海軍の軍艦と貨物
船の衝突事件は４件もありました。そのうちの２件で、17人もの
水兵が死亡しているのです。

The Obama administration made redoing the military in a political
correct fashion one of it's priorities. Trans sexual people were allowed
to serve. Trans sexual people, racial minorities and women were given
preference in promotion.

先述した通り、オバマ政権がポリティカル・コレクトネスで軍隊

187

Chapter6 Where America is headed, and what Japan should do

を作り直すことを、優先事項の一つとしました。性転換をした人も、軍への入隊を許可されました。性転換した人、民族的なマイノリティ、そして女性の昇進が優先されるようになりました。

Any small perceived insult by a heterosexual white male military member is grounds for dismissal. Officers are more concerned with protecting their careers than arguing against this policy. In fact, when President Obama assumed office, he fired some 197 military officers, mostly for disagreeing with his polices.

異性愛者の白人男性がする話が侮辱的だと感じられたら、それはそのまま解雇の理由になります。士官たちは、こうした政策に反対するよりも、自分のキャリアの方が大切です。そもそもオバマ氏が大統領になった時に、彼の政策に同意しない士官 197 人を解雇しています。

So many competent white military people have quit. The people who have risen to replace them are not competent at their jobs. The result is a military that cannot perform well.

それで、数多くの有能な軍人が辞任し、その後任として配属された人たちが、仕事をこなせる能力がない人たちであったことは、先に述べた通りです。結果は、無能力な軍隊です。

Who can craft a solution?
誰が事態を収束させるのか

In the case of civil disorder in America, there be a crucial point where the remaining competent military people, and the truth is they are mostly white, some not white, will desert over to the militia.

第6章　アメリカの今後と日本の進むべき道

　アメリカ国内が大混乱となった場合の重要なポイントは、軍隊に
残っている有能な人材は、そのほとんどが白人であり、残る少数が
白人以外であるということと、このような能力的に優れた人たちは、
民兵組織へと脱走するだろうということです。

The only thing preventing this form happening is the existence of
President Trump. People forget that militia organizations like the
Oathkeepers and the III%ers threatened to march on Washington if Hillary
Clinton had become President. Their leaders declared her unacceptable.

　現在、トランプ大統領の存在だけが、このような事態を止めてい
ます。アメリカの人々が忘れていることは、もしヒラリー・クリン
トン氏が大統領になっていたら、民兵組織である「オース・キーパー
ズ」と「III%ers」がワシントンに抗議の行進をするという宣言を
していたことです。彼らのリーダーは、クリントン氏を容認できな
いと明言していました。

Looking at videos of the Charlottesville incident, I was impressed by the
Oathkeepers. They conducted themselves well in a tense situation. With
discipline. And they are well armed. On the other hand, the Antifa are
little better than a mob.

　私は、シャーロッツビル事件の動画を見て、オース・キーパーズ
に感銘を受けました。彼らは、あのような緊迫した状況でも、うま
く活動していました。彼らは規律を持っています。武器もたくさん
持っています。逆に言えば、反ファシズム運動の人たちは、ただの
群衆です。

Somewhere, sometime a US military general is going to get tired of the
mess, and take over. This solution is becoming more and more likely. The
militia movement will support this, and so will the Right wing Christian
Fundamentalist movement.

189

Chapter6 Where America is headed, and what Japan should do

いつか、どこかで、一人の米軍の将軍が、このメチャクチャな混乱にうんざりして、天下を取るかもしれません。その可能性が、だんだんと高まっています。民兵組織も、右派のキリスト教原理主義の人たちも、これを支持するでしょう。

There will be a political crackdown in America. Actually, critical articles about the Antifa are beginning to appear in major media, like the Wall Street Journal and the Washington Post. Since the media is controlled by only a few major corporations, they can be considered part of the Deep State, and would be easy to control.

今後アメリカでは、政治的な締めつけが強まるでしょう。実際、マスメディアでも、例えば、ウォール・ストリート・ジャーナルとワシントン・ポストに、反ファシズム運動に対する批判的な記事が現れています。そもそも、マスメディアが大手の数社だけで支配されているからこそ、ディープ・ステートの一部として、簡単に操ることができるのです。

But even so, there will be a need for many arrests to bring Antifa and Black Lives Matter under control. Particularly in the case of the Antifa, they have a secret underground organization. It will be extremely difficult to eliminate them. And since the basic causes of unrest, such as the wealth gap, still exist in America, it will probably not be possible without destroying them in a Civil War.

それでも、反ファシズム運動やブラック・ライヴズ・マターの組織をコントロールするためには、さらに多くの人を逮捕する必要があります。特に、反ファシズム運動の場合には、秘密の地下組織があります。こうした組織を完全に排除することは、非常に困難です。そして、アメリカには社会的な混乱の根本的な原因、例えば格差問題のようなものがまだあり、このようなグループを、内乱で消す以外の方法で排除することは、かなり難しいでしょう。

190

第6章 アメリカの今後と日本の進むべき道

The Left will respond with riots demanding their Rights. But the Left will be crushed in the ensuing crackdown. It will be based on politics and religion. And the America that results from this will be very different from what we know today.

　左派の反動は、自分たちの権利を要求するための暴動なのでしょうが、しかし、その後の取り締まりで、左派は壊滅します。この取り締まりの根拠は、政治と、宗教上の信念です。内乱後のアメリカは、現在のアメリカとは全く違うアメリカになるでしょう。

The Left can't see reality
左派には真実が見えていない

The Left does not seem to realize this at all. I have read some accounts giving the Left the advantage in the coming conflict, because they control the media.

　左派は、こうした真実を全く理解していません。私は、これからの内乱では左派が有利であるという記事を読みました。なぜなら、彼ら左派がマスメディアを支配しているからです。

No. And the Left is focusing on attacking history, such as statues of Confederate generals. And on attacking Right wing demonstrators. Yes, it is true that the Far Right is a little nuts. But they are a tiny minority.

　でも、それは間違いです。左派は歴史を破壊すること、例えば南北戦争の将軍の記念碑を排除することに焦点を当てています。そして右派のデモを行う人たちを攻撃しています。まあ、確かに極右派というのは、ちょっとおかしい人が多いのですが、しかし、彼らは数少ない少数派です。

191

Chapter6 Where America is headed, and what Japan should do

Even in Japan we have a Nazi party. I think they have 20 members. We ignore them.

日本にもナチス党はあります。でも、メンバーは20人くらいでしょう。普通の日本人は、彼らを無視しています。

The true power of the Right lies in the Christian Fundamentalist movement and the militia movement. And the Left does not see it.

アメリカの右派の本当の力は、キリスト教原理主義者と民兵組織にあります。左派には、この真実が見えていません。

When they move, and the Left make their usual screaming demands, some of the Left will be shot outright. Many will be rounded up and deported to work farms in the country.

そうした本当の右派が活動を始めた場合、左派がいつものように自分たちの要求を叫んでいると、何人かはそのまま撃たれるでしょう。多くの左派が一勢に検挙されて、田舎の労働農場へ送られます。

The special snowflakes of the Left will not be able to bear this, and many will die from shock.

しかし左派のデリケートな「特別な雪片」たちが、このようなことに耐えられるわけがなく、彼らの多くはショックで死ぬでしょう。

Unfortunately this will be the end of American intellectual life, and the end of America as a technological society. Some commentators I have read doubt that America will be able to maintain nationwide electric power.

残念ながら、この内乱によって、アメリカの理知的な人たちは消え、テクノロジーの時代も終わります。私が読んだ、ある評論家の記事によれば、内乱後のアメリカでは、国内全土で電力を維持することができるかどうかすら、疑いの余地があるとのことです。

第6章 アメリカの今後と日本の進むべき道

It is no longer safe for the American Right to hold a political rally, always the Antifa shows up and attacks. Civil War is inevitable.

アメリカの右派が行う集会には、もはや安全はなく、常に反ファシズム運動の者が現れて暴力的な攻撃を受ける可能性があります。もう、内乱は避けられないのです。

And make no mistake, for America it is going to be bad, real bad. Civil Wars always are.

そして、間違いなく、アメリカにとってこの内乱は、本当に酷いことになるでしょう。内乱とは、常にそういうものです。

The role of America as the world's policeman, and leading nation, will be gone for many decades.

世界の警察官、世界のリーダーとしてのアメリカの役割は、今後何十年にもわたって、なくなってしまうのです。

What should Japan do?
日本の進むべき道

So what should Japan do?

では、日本はどうしたら良いのでしょうか？

As a first measure, we must purify our nation. Too many people believe that any kind of philosophy or idea coming out of America is wonderful. No.

まず最初に、日本を浄化する必要があります。日本人の中には、アメリカから出て来るものなら、どんな哲学や提案でも素晴らしい、

193

Chapter6 Where America is headed, and what Japan should do

と信じている人が多すぎます。でも違います。そうではありません。

For example, let's look at the concept of diversity. Many Japanese believe everything that Americans say about diversity. Well, to tell you the truth, Americans have a habit of playing word games, they just say something and pretend it is truth.

例えば、多様性という概念について見てみましょう。多くの日本人は、アメリカ人が多様性について話す内容を、すべて信じてしまいます。でも正直に言うと、アメリカ人には言葉遊びのクセがあり、ただ単に何かを発言して、それを、さも真実であるかのように見せようとする傾向があります。

In American education, diversity is encouraged, unity is discouraged. Of the protests occurring today on America's streets, the Left is constantly attacking White Privilege. This is the concept that white people have an unfair advantage in society, which allows them to profit more than minorities.

アメリカの教育では、多様性は奨励され、統一性は妨害されます。現在、アメリカの街なかで行われている抗議では、左派は常に、白人特権に対する攻撃をしています。これは、アメリカ社会の中では、白人が不公平に有利な特権を持ち、だから少数派（マイノリティ）よりも良い生活ができる、いう考え方です。

These Americans tell us in Japan that we are not diverse enough, we need to import more different kinds of people. This will make Japan stronger. No, the opposite is true. By creating separate identities for minorities, particularly Black Americans, America has created a permanent group of people who are not Americans. They are first Black people, not American, and that is now how they think and react.

こうしたアメリカ人たちは、日本には多様性が足りないと言い、

194

第6章　アメリカの今後と日本の進むべき道

日本をより強くするためには様々な種類の外国人を受け入れる必要
があると言います。しかし本当は逆です。アメリカは少数派、特に
黒人のために別のアイデンティティを作り出し、それによって永遠
にアメリカ人ではないグループを作り出しました。彼らはまず第一
に「黒人」であって、「アメリカ人」ではない、そのように考えて
行動します。

I hear many voices saying that we should import more foreign workers,
since the birth rate is falling. In my neighborhood, there are many people
from a certain South Asian country. But what can they do here? In
convenience stores, they can only perform the most simple tasks. Their
Japanese language ability is low. When I went to pay for something I
ordered on the net, they cannot understand my Japanese, they say it isn't
here. It was there, I had to get a person who spoke Japanese.

　日本では、出生率が低いから外国人労働者が必要である、と言っ
ている人もいます。私の家の近所に、ある南アジアの国の人がたく
さん住んでいます。しかし、この日本で、彼らに何ができるでしょ
うか？　コンビニエンスストアでも、最も簡単な仕事しかできませ
ん。彼らの日本語力は低いです。私がネットで注文した物の代金を
支払いに行った際には、私の日本語を理解できず、「そのような物
はない」と言いました。その時も、ちゃんとした日本語が話せる店
員が必要であると実感しました。

Recently, on a whim, I went to a Spanish restaurant near my house. The
staff was completely from that South Asian country. These guys proudly
told me how they had worked in Spanish restaurants in Japan, and decided
to make their own place. But the service was terrible. The food was over
priced. To understand Japanese concepts of service, it takes about 10 years
at least. And at least that long to learn the Japanese language enough to be
competent.

　先日も、きまぐれに、家の近くにあるスペイン・レストランへ行っ

195

Chapter6 Where America is headed, and what Japan should do

てみました。その店のスタッフは全員、その南アジアの国から来た人たちでした。彼らは、日本にある別のスペイン・レストランで働いていたことを誇らしげに語り、それで今度は自分たちのレストランを作ることに決めたのだと語りました。しかし、サービスはひどかったですし、料金も高かったです。日本のサービスを理解するまでには、最低でも 10 年はかかるでしょう。また、有能に働けるようになるには、ちゃんとした日本語を学ぶために、やはり同じくらいの時間がかかるでしょう。

Many foreigners will disagree with me here, but I come from another country, I know. And there also is the way of thinking. I completely identify as Japanese. Everything I do at work, I think and act as a Japanese. That is the only way to succeed here.

このことについて、ほとんどの外国人が私に同意しません。しかし、私は他国で生まれ、この問題を分かっています。だから、私は完全に日本人と同化します。仕事をする時も、常に日本人として考え、日本人として活動しています。日本で成功するためには、その方法しかないのです。

A flood of American refugees
押し寄せるアメリカからの難民

People who tell us we should have social diversity, well why should we lower standards and change our society to fit some foreigners? Look at America, all this talk of diversity has produced riots where people fight in the streets. Soon, they will kill each other.

日本の社会には多様性が必要であると言う人がいますが、なぜ基準を下げてまで、少数の外国人のために社会を変える必要があるのでしょうか？ アメリカを見てください。この多様性の結果、街な

196

第6章　アメリカの今後と日本の進むべき道

かで人が戦っています。そのうちには、お互いを殺し始めます。

That is not something I wish for Japan. Visa regulations should be tightened. For Permanent Resident permits, Japanese speaking and reading should be required. Also, a test of Japanese culture and history.

私は、日本にそのようなことになってほしくないです。入国ビザの基準は、もっと厳しくするべきです。永住権を許可する場合、日本語を読み書きする能力は必須にするべきです。それと、日本の文化と歴史の理解度を見るための試験をするべきです。

Foreigners who cannot function in Japanese society will become permanent wards of the state. And they will riot. When I see so many people from this one country in my neighborhood, I despair. The husbands will learn some Japanese language, but the wives will never learn Japanese. The children go to a school in their own language. They will not assimilate well into Japanese society, and cannot go back to their home country, they will become rootless people. And they will become a criminal and political problem in Japan.

日本の社会に適合できない外国人は、永遠に国から福祉をもらっている人になります。こうした人たちは、いずれ暴動を起こします。自分の家の近所にたくさん住んでいる、こうした外国人たちを見ると、私は絶望を感じます。彼らのうち、夫の方は何とか日本語を覚えますが、奥さんの方は絶対に日本語が上手くなりません。子供たちは、自分たちの国語の学校へ行きます。彼らは日本社会に同化せず、かといって自分の祖国に戻ることもできない、根のない人々になります。そしてだんだんと、犯罪を行い、政治的な問題を起こすグループになるのです。

In the near future, we will also have many refugees from America coming to Japan. There has been much international marriage between Americans and Japanese. Most of them live in the United States.

197

Chapter6 Where America is headed, and what Japan should do

近い将来、多くの難民がアメリカから日本に来るでしょう。これまでも、アメリカ人と日本人の国際結婚は、数多くありました。でも、こうした人たちは、ほとんどがアメリカに住んでいます。

As America descends into chaos and collapse, many of them will get the idea that they should return to Japan. But what can they do here? We will have no more need of English conversation teachers, there are already too many here.

しかし、今後アメリカがだんだん混乱に陥って崩壊し始めると、この、国際結婚をした多くの人たちは、日本に住むことを考えるようになります。しかし、日本で彼らに何ができますか？ 英会話の先生は必要ありません。今でも多すぎるくらいです。

And by being American, they will have strong attitudes about their self importance, and will be very forceful in expressing their views.

しかも彼らはアメリカ人ですから、自分のことを尊大に考え、自分の意見を強く主張します。

They will say things like "I am an architect, I want to use my skills in Japan". The problem is, we already have many Japanese architects. In fact, in any technical area, Japanese people are the most competent in the world. There is nothing more the West can teach us.

例えば、「私は建築家だ。私の技術を日本で使いたい」というアメリカ人が、難民として日本に入国したとします。問題は、日本にもすでに数多くの建築家がいるということです。それに、実際のところ、どのような分野においても、技術的なことでは日本人が世界一です。もはや西洋の国から教わることなどありません。

The problem is, the foreign people in my neighborhood are not Japanese. Even though it will be tough, we can send them back to their country. But in the case of American refugee families, the wife will be

198

第6章　アメリカの今後と日本の進むべき道

Japanese, and the children will have the right to Japanese citizenship. The husband will have the right to a working visa.

　先ほど取り上げた、私の近所に住む外国人たちは、日本人ではありません。だから、大変でも、自分の国へ返すことができます。しかし、アメリカ難民の家族の場合、奥さんは日本国民です。子供たちは日本国籍を得る権利があります。アメリカ人の夫も、日本で就労ビザを受け取る権利があります。

So we cannot simply turn them away. But their language skills will be very poor, culturally, they will think like Americans, and that will not work well in Japan.

　だから、簡単に彼らの入国を拒否することはできません。しかし、この人たちの日本語力は低く、文化的にもアメリカ人のように考える人たちです。日本では上手くいきません。

So I propose this to the Japanese government. Let us set up a program that will send these people to rural districts in Japan. We can set up a program where experienced farmers oversee the new people, and teach them farming, forestry, or fishing.

　ここで私は、日本政府に提案をします。このような人たちを、日本の地方に送るプログラムを作りましょう。新しい機関を作って、経験豊富な農家の人たちが、このような新しく来た人たちに農業、林業、漁業などを教え、彼らがそこで働けるように育てるのです。

Well, as I have written, Americans are full of self importance. But there is no other place in Japan for for them. And for those who demand they be treated specially, and there will be such people, I propose we develop Japanese run farms in Russian Siberia. We can send the difficult ones there. They will learn the true meaning of work.

　先にも書いたように、アメリカ人は自分のことを尊大に考える人

199

Chapter6 Where America is headed, and what Japan should do

が多いです。しかし日本には、他に彼らのための場所がありません。それから、彼らの中には、自分だけを特別扱いするように要求する人が絶対にいます。私はロシアのシベリアに、日本経営の農場を開発することを提案します。そうすれば、そういう難しい人たちを、そこへ送ることができます。そこで彼らは、働くことの本当の意味を学ぶでしょう。

How can American refugees live in Japan
アメリカ難民と日本人の共存

Some people will be surprised at what I am saying here. But this is true. For a long time, Americans have grown up with the concept that they deserve total satisfaction, simply by being born American.

こうした私の提案に、驚く人もいるでしょう。しかし、ここに書いたことは本当です。アメリカ人は、ただアメリカ人として生まれたという理由だけで、完璧な満足を得られなければならないという発想で育っています。

That is not true, and it is not in American philosophy. In the Declaration of Independence, it guarantees "The right to the pursuit of happiness". It guarantees that you can attempt to achieve happiness. That your race or gender or circumstances of birth will not prevent you from achieving happiness. It does not guarantee that you will succeed.

でも、それは間違っています。そんなことはアメリカの哲学に入っていません。確かに、先にも述べたように、アメリカの独立宣言で、「幸福を追求する権利」を保証しています。これは、人が幸福になることを追求することを保証する、という意味です。民族、性別、生まれた環境によって、その幸福が妨げられることはない、という保証なのです。彼らが成功することまでは保証していません。

200

第6章　アメリカの今後と日本の進むべき道

But over the years, Americans have misinterpreted this as a guarantee of success. No. There is the concept of responsible, and irresponsible citizenship.

しかし長年にわたって、アメリカ人は独立宣言のこのフレーズを、みずからの成功の保証であると誤解しています。でも違います。そこには、責任を持った市民権と、責任を持っていない市民権という概念があります。

Responsible citizenship means that you realize you are part of a community, and you have to cooperate and live with others. Irresponsible citizenship means that you are always demanding your own complete satisfaction, and do not care about anyone else.

責任を持った市民権というのは、あなたはコミュニティの中の一人であることを理解して、他人と協力し、一緒に生活する必要がある、という意味です。一方、責任を持っていない市民権というのは、あなたは常に自分の完璧な満足を要求しているだけであり、他人のことなど考えていない、という意味です。

An example. I moved to my present neighborhood some years ago. The local housewives have a garbage rule. That rule is garbage must be put out in the early morning of the day of collection, not the night before. Where I previously lived, in the same ward in Tokyo, I always put the garbage out the previous evening. Frankly, the ward does recommend putting out garbage in the morning. But it is only a recommendation, not a hard and fast rule. In my previous neighborhood, it was not a problem.

例えば、こういうことです。私は、いま住んでいる場所に数年前に引っ越してきました。近所の主婦たちには、ゴミ出しのルールがあります。そのルールは、ゴミは収集日の朝に出す、前日の夜に出してはいけない、というものです。私が前に住んでいた場所では、それは東京の同じ区の中でしたが、いつもゴミを前日の夜に出して

201

いました。正直に言えば、区では、朝に出すことを勧めています。しかし、あくまで推奨であり、厳密なルールではありません。なので、前に住んでいた所では、これは問題になりませんでした。

But in my new neighborhood has a custom that the local housewives enforce the ward recommendation strongly. If I were to act like a typical American, I would demand my rights, I would say that there is no law to put the garbage out in the morning. I would be the cause of social unrest in my neighborhood, because of the garbage.

しかし、いま住んでいる場所では、主婦たちが、推奨されていることをきちんと実施しています。ここで私が普通のアメリカ人の態度をとるなら、あくまで自分の権利を主張して、ゴミを朝に出す法律などないと主張するでしょう。このようにして私は、ゴミの問題をめぐる社会闘争の原因になります。

That is ridiculous. I have lived in Japan now more than 40 years. It is much better to get along with your neighbors, than insist on your own way. And you never know, maybe some day you will need your neighbor's help.

これは愚かなことです。私は日本に40年以上、住んでいます。自分のやり方を主張することより、近所の皆さんと仲良くすることの方が大切です。それに、もしかしたら、いつか近所の人たちの助けが必要になるかもしれないのです。

Japanese people do respect people who work hard or make strong effort. No matter where they may be born. But those people born in other countries must make the effort, not give up part way and say "In my country, this is how things are done, I should have social recognition for behaving as in my country of birth!"

日本人は、一生懸命に働く人、努力する人を尊敬します。生まれた場所や国は関係ありません。しかし、そうした海外で生まれた人

第6章　アメリカの今後と日本の進むべき道

たちも、本当の努力をするべきであり、途中であきらめて、「私の
国では、こういうやり方なのです。私は、この自分の生まれた国の
やり方で社会的に認められるべきなのです！」などと言ってはダメ
なのです。

Those born elsewhere must become Japanese, there is no other way.

　別の場所、別の国で生まれた人たちは日本人になる必要があり、
他の方法はありません。

The LGBT issue in Japan
日本におけるＬＧＢＴの問題

LGBT means lesbian, gay, bisexual, and trans sexual. It is used to refer
to problems for people who fall into this category.

　ＬＧＢＴとは、女性の同性愛者、男性の同性愛者、両性愛者、お
よびトランスジェンダーの、英語の頭文字をつなげたものであり、
こうした人たちの抱える問題を指します。

As far as LGBT, that is Gay problems, for Japan this is not a problem.
Some people want to make laws protecting Gay people in Japan. This
is not at all necessary. America is a country where Gays were hunted.
Sometimes they were killed, usually just humiliated.

　ＬＧＢＴについて、特にゲイに関する問題のことですが、日本の
場合には、これはそれほど問題ではありません。何人かの人たちが、
ゲイの人を守るための法律を作ろうとしていますが、これは必ずし
も必要ではありません。一方、アメリカは、ゲイの人たちが狩られ
ていたような国です。時には殺されることもあり、たいていは屈辱
的な仕打ちを受けました。

203

Chapter6 Where America is headed, and what Japan should do

This has never been the case in Japan. Japan has always had a vibrant Gay culture. I have worked for many years in Yamanashi Prefecture, and Takeda Shingen, the Daimyo from the warring states era, is a hero there. It is well known that he was Gay, or at least bi-sexual, but it is not an issue there.

でも、日本では、そのようなことはありませんでした。日本では昔から、ゲイ・カルチャー（男色文化）というものがありました。私は長年、山梨県で働いていましたが、戦国時代の大名、武田信玄は地元の英雄です。彼がゲイ、あるいは両性愛者だということは、皆が知っていますが、そのことはたいした問題ではありません。

The Trans gender problem is a different story. These are people who do not fit their physical bodies. It is a mental health issue. In America, Left wing activists are using these people to destroy the existence of the State. That is why they are demanding so many special rights for them.

トランスジェンダーの問題は、これとは別の問題です。この人たちは、心の性別が肉体の性別に合っていません。彼らの場合は、メンタル・ヘルス、つまり精神衛生上の問題です。しかしアメリカでは、左派の活動家がこうした人たちを、国を崩壊させるために利用しています。そのために、トランスジェンダーの人のための、特別な権利を要求しています。

We should not fall into this trap in Japan. I have friends who have spoken to Gay people in Shinjuku, the famous 2 chome night town area for Gays. They do not like all this political and social attention. We should leave them alone.

日本の人たちは、こうしたワナに陥らない方が良いです。私の友達が、新宿2丁目の夜のゲイの街へ行って、ゲイの人たちの話を聞いてきました。彼らは、社会的、政治的に注目されることを嫌っています。彼らは、そのままそっとしておくべきです。

Trans gender people need mental health counseling. But we should not change society around, by declaring uni sex toilets for example, to satisfy a few activists. And even if we do that, these activists will demand something more.

心と体の性別が違うトランスジェンダーの人には、精神的なカウンセリングが必要です。しかし、数人の活動家の満足のために、例えば、全国にユニセックス（男女共用）のトイレを作るというように、社会を変えるべきではありません。そのようなことを実現しても、その活動家たちは、さらに別の何かを要求するだけです。

Economic policy after the American collapse
アメリカ崩壊後の経済政策

Now we come to some important areas that the collapse of America will bring about. Japan is heavily dependent on trade with the United States. We will have to consider that it will be interrupted for a considerable period of time, perhaps several decades, while a new America arises.

アメリカの崩壊が日本にもたらす影響の中で、非常に重要な分野があります。日本は、アメリカとの貿易に大きく依存しています。新しいアメリカが立ち上がるまでの長い期間、おそらく数十年にわたって、この貿易が途絶えるということを考えなければならないでしょう。

A large portion of our food supply comes from America. We can no longer depend on this. We must make a national effort to increase Japanese food production. Many people will lose their jobs because of the economic ramifications of the American civil war. We should move these people to rural farming and fishing districts. This will help to revive local areas. And give us the possibility of feeding ourselves.

Chapter6 Where America is headed, and what Japan should do

日本の多くの食料は、アメリカから輸入しています。しかしこれからは、それらに依存することはできません。ですから、日本国内の食料生産を増やすように、全国で努力をする必要があります。アメリカの内乱による経済の混乱によって、多くの日本人が仕事を失います。この人たちを移動させて、地方での農業や漁業にあたらせるべきです。これによって地方を活性化できます。そして、日本の食料自給率を上げ、自分で自分の国をまかなう、自給自足の可能性を求めましょう。

Also, we should begin talks with Russia about having Japanese people in Siberia to build farms there. I think the Russians will welcome this.

また、ロシアと話をして、シベリアに日本人を送り、そこで農場を作る計画を進めるべきです。おそらくロシアは、この提案を歓迎するでしょう。

Many people in Japan will be shocked when I say cooperate with Russia. There are still some bitter memories of the The Great Pacific War, or the Northern Territories issue.

この話をすると、多くの日本人が、ロシアと協力することに驚きます。大東亜戦争や北方領土をめぐる悲惨な歴史から、ロシアに対して苦い思いを持っているのでしょう。

But I say we should look at reality. America has since the end of The Great Pacific War, been the guarantor of Japan's existence. Because of internal strife, that will no longer be possible.

しかし、現実を見ましょう。大東亜戦争の終結からのち、アメリカは日本の保証人となってきました。しかし国内の内紛によって、それはもはや不可能になりました。

Russia has a sometimes good, sometimes bad relationship with China. But their reality is, Siberia is a long way from Moscow. A large part of the

第6章　アメリカの今後と日本の進むべき道

population of Siberia is Chinese. I think they would welcome Japanese investment and settlement there.

　ロシアは中国と、つかず離れずの関係を続けています。ロシアという国の現実として、シベリアはモスクワから遠い場所です。しかも今、シベリアには、多くの中国人が住んでいます。ロシア人たちは、シベリアへの日本人の移住、投資を歓迎するでしょう。

This is beneficial for Japan, and geopolitical reality. And it would give us a land ally on the Asian continent with a powerful army. Something we should think deeply about. After all, Americans were bitter enemies during The Great Pacific War, but since then we have grown into a deep friendship. We can do the same with Russia.

　これは日本にとっても有益な、地政学上の現実です。これによって日本は、アジア大陸で力を持つ陸軍の同盟国ができるのです。こうしたことを、日本人は深く考えた方が良いでしょう。何といっても、大東亜戦争で敵として戦ったアメリカと日本は、その戦争のあとに深い交友関係を結んでいます。きっとロシアとも同じことができます。

TPP was not about Free Trade
ＴＰＰは自由な貿易ではない

Very unfortunately, Prime Minister Abe has shown himself to be rather naive about Americans, particularly in business. In Japanese society there is the concept of Giri and Ninjyo, Basically, Giri is obligation, to those above you, for example your boss. Ninjyo is the feeling that you should take care of the people below you.

　残念ながら、現在の安倍総理は、特にビジネスの分野で、アメリ

207

Chapter6 Where America is headed, and what Japan should do

カ人に対して甘いです。日本の社会には、義理と人情という規範が
あります。基本的に、義理は、自分の上司などに感じる恩義のこと、
人情は、自分の下の者に対する思いやりのこと、と言えるかもしれ
ません。

When I saw Japan negotiate the TPP treaty, I was very anxious about
how naive the Japanese side was about American intentions. Americans
just don't have the same feelings about work as Japanese do. For the
American worker, they only work if they are getting paid for every little
thing. There is no such thing as job security in America. A company will
fire some one very easily to save money, even if he was a loyal employee.

日本がTPP条約の交渉をしている時も、日本側がアメリカ側の
意図に対して本当に甘いので、私はとても心配でした。アメリカ人
は、仕事というものに対して、日本人と同じ考え方をしていません。
アメリカの労働者の場合、どんな些細なことでも、お金をもらわな
いと、仕事をしません。また、アメリカでは、仕事の安定性はなく、
たとえ忠実な従業員でも、コスト削減のために、いとも簡単に解雇
されます。

TPP was not about free trade, the rules were set so that a very few rich
Americans would win. No one else would benefit at all. It did not benefit
the average American, or Japanese person, in any way. That is why
President Trump cancelled it.

TPPには、自由貿易というような意味はありませんでした。ひ
と握りのお金持ちのアメリカ人が勝つようなルールが設定されてい
ました。彼ら以外には、誰も利益を受けられません。一般的なアメ
リカ人も、日本人も、得られる利益はゼロでした。こうした理由で、
トランプ大統領はTPPから脱退しました。

Rich Americans do not care at all about the people who work for them.
This is why America is now in revolt. This is in contrast to an earlier age

208

where great Americans who became rich like Dale Carnegie or Cornelius Vanderbilt engaged in philanthropy, to help others.

　お金持ちのアメリカ人たちは、自分の下で働いている人たちのことを全く考えていません。そのことが、今アメリカが反乱にさらされ、革命状態になってきている理由なのです。これは、例えば、デール・カーネギー氏やコーネリアス・ヴァンダービルト氏のような、お金持ちでありながら慈善事業にも携わった、かつての偉大なアメリカ人とは対照的です。

Unfortunately, some Japanese are now doing business like Americans. The part time worker, or Haken business has become an inescapable living hell for the people in it.

　残念なことに、一部の日本人はアメリカ人のようなやり方でビジネスを行っています。アルバイトや派遣社員といった立場の人たちは、一生その地位から逃げられない、地獄のような生活をしています。

And Japan has adapted excessive student loans, that cannot be paid back. By destroying students, we destroy the future of the nation.

　そして現在、日本には、過度な学生ローンというものが定着し、学生たちはそれを返済できていません。国が学生を潰すことは、国の将来を潰すことにつながります。

We will have to find a more fair way of work, and ensuring education.

　私たちは、もっと公正に仕事を探すための方法、確実に教育を受けるための方法を見つけなければなりません。

Chapter 7

The problems of Defense after the collapse of America
アメリカ崩壊後の防衛問題

The crucial need to expand the Self Defense Forces
自衛隊の増強が不可欠

Defence. This is a serious issue. The US Navy and the other military services have guaranteed world order for many years in the Pacific. Yet they are overstretched, do not have enough ships, and are plagued with political correctness problems.

防衛、これは重要な問題です。アメリカ海軍とその他の軍隊は、長年にわたり、太平洋における世界秩序を守ってきました。しかし、守るべき場所は広大で、軍艦は足りず、ポリティカル・コレクトネスの問題にも悩まされています。

Every year, 16% of the women on US Navy ships must be removed because of pregnancy. Often they are not replaced, other crew members must take their place. Crews are overworked, often going days with little sleep. Instruction in basics like seamanship and navigation has been eliminated, officers are handed DVD's for self study.

先にも述べたように、毎年アメリカ海軍の軍艦の女性乗組員の16％が妊婦になり、産休のために任務を交代しなければなりません。しかし多くの場合、任務を代わることは不可能で、別の乗組員がその人の分も仕事をする必要があります。そのため、乗組員は働きすぎの状態になり、何日間も睡眠不足が続きます。船舶の操縦と

第7章 アメリカ崩壊後の防衛問題

航海の教育をする余裕もなく、新人の士官は、独学で勉強するためのＤＶＤを海軍からもらっているようなありさまです。

As political problems in the US increase, it could divide ship crews, making them non functional.

アメリカで国内政治の問題が高まれば、軍艦の乗組員たちも考え方の違いによって分断されてしまい、艦が機能不全に陥る可能性があります。

It may be necessary for Japan to be the protector of Hawaii and Alaska for a time, to prevent some other power from seizing them.

もしかすると、ハワイとアラスカを他国に侵略されないように、日本が守る必要に迫られるかもしれません。

In any case it will be necessary to greatly expand the Navy, Army and Air Force. We will have to draw a defense arc from the straits of Malacca to Alaska and Hawaii. There will still be some American forces available, but until political and social chaos in the US is resolved, we cannot be sure how many forces can be committed.

いずれにせよ、日本の海上、陸上、航空自衛隊を、大幅に拡大する必要が出てくるでしょう。マラッカ海峡からハワイ、アラスカに防衛線を引いて、それらを守る必要があります。その際、利用できるいくつかのアメリカ軍の部隊や軍艦も、少しはあるでしょう。しかし、アメリカ国内の混乱が解決するまで、どのくらいのアメリカ軍部隊が利用できるのかは未知数です。

I think in Japan we should prepare for America to be militarily incapable, or only able to field reduced forces for at least 15 years. It took that long to recover from the disaster of the Vietnam war.

日本は、アメリカ軍が軍事的な機能不全に陥ること、あるいは、

211

Chapter7 The problems of Defense after the collapse of America

少なくとも 15 年くらいは、限られた数少ない部隊だけで戦うよう
になることを、想定しておいた方が良いと思います。ベトナム戦争
の失敗から回復するためには、そのくらいの時間がかかりました。

But after the Vietnam war, internally America was at peace. Not this
time. So we may be looking at 30 or 40 years where Japan must take the
main role in the Pacific.

とはいえ、ベトナム戦争後に関して言えば、アメリカ国内は平和
な状態でした。しかし、今は違います。そうなると、日本が太平洋
で軍事上の中心的な役割を果たさなければならない期間は、30 ～
40 年になるかもしれません。

We will have to build more ships of all types, develop Naval Aviation,
more carriers, subs, surface combatants.

海上自衛隊は、これからあらゆる種類の艦艇を、さらに造船する
必要があるでしょう。その上で、海軍航空部隊を創設し、空母、潜
水艦、水上戦闘艦艇も、さらに必要になります。

We will need to expand the Army, and create a Marine Corps of at least
two divisions.

陸上自衛隊もさらに拡大し、二個師団くらいの海兵隊も創設する
必要があるでしょう。

We will need produce our own combat aircraft, both defensive fighters
and strike aircraft. And cruise missiles.

それと、日本も独自の戦闘機、攻撃機を生産する必要があります。
それに加えて、巡航ミサイルも生産するべきです。

And we need to make a Japanese Intelligence Service. This will be
essential. Take a look at our main rival, China. They do not like American

power in Japan. If that power were to fail, they would then attempt to dominate Japan for themselves.

　そして、日本の情報部局（諜報機関）の確立は、絶対に必要です。これは非常に重要です。日本の一番のライバルである中国を注視してください。彼らは、日本にアメリカの力が入っていることを嫌います。そのアメリカの力がなくなった場合、自分の国益のために、迷わず日本を支配しようとするでしょう。

An Intelligence Agency would be instrumental in determining Chinese intentions, and perhaps influencing Chinese actions to Japan's benefit.

　情報部局（諜報機関）は、こうした中国の計画を察知すること、あるいは日本の国益のために中国の活動に影響を与えることが、非常に重要です。

Intelligence Agencies can prevent wars. I know. My own experience was as a Naval Intelligence agent inside an American Communist Party spy group in Iwakuni, Yamaguchi Prefecture, a US Marine base.

　情報部局（諜報機関）は戦争を防ぐことが可能です。私はそれを、自分の経験から知っています。私の任務は、山口県岩国市にある米海兵隊基地の、アメリカ共産主義スパイグループに対するスパイ活動でした。

The American Communist party was trying to use the anti Vietnam war movement in the US to force American withdrawal from South Korea. Then North Korea would have a free chance to attack the South.

　アメリカの共産党は、ベトナム戦争の反戦運動を利用して、米軍が韓国から撤退するように仕向け、その後、北朝鮮が自由に韓国に攻撃ができるような状態を作ろうとしていました。

I call it "The Second Korean War". The Communist effort failed, it

213

Chapter7 The problems of Defense after the collapse of America

never became a hot war, but remained a shadow war.

私は、これを「第二次朝鮮戦争」と呼んでいます。共産主義者に
よる計画が失敗して、本当の戦争にはなりませんでしたので、影の
戦争のまま終わりました。

That is part of what Intelligence Agencies do.

このようなことは、情報部局（諜報機関）の活動の一部です。

Article No.9 does not protect Japan
憲法9条は日本を守ってくれない

Now my Japanese Leftist friends are going to scream about the
Constitution and Article number 9. I have lived in Japan for 43 years and
have had this conversation too many times. One thing, a piece of paper is
not going to defend the country from enemies, and we do have them.

私の、日本人の左派の友達は、日本の憲法9条のことについて、
声高に語ります。私は日本に43年間住んで、何度もこうした会話
をしてきました。一つ、紙で書いた文章は、敵から国を守りません。
そして、日本には敵国が存在します。

Yes, the Constitution has kept us from getting involved in American
land wars in Asia, like Vietnam, and that is a good thing. But times
change. American power will now diminish rapidly, we must prepare.

まあ、この憲法があったために、アメリカが起こしたアジアでの
地上戦、例えばベトナム戦争に日本は参加しませんでした。それは
良いことです。しかし、時代は変わります。これから、アメリカの
力は急速に弱まります。私たちは準備をしなければなりません。

第 7 章　アメリカ崩壊後の防衛問題

And the Constitution has never ever protected Japan since WWII. Japan has been protected by a combination of Japanese military power, the Self Defense Forces, and American power based in Japan.

大東亜戦争の終結以来、憲法が日本を守ったことはありません。日本を守ったのは、自衛隊と在日米軍のコンビです。

Many people in Japan who have Leftist beliefs think that by having a military we will attract war. The opposite is true. In recent years, we have seen China simply take over the islands of various countries in the South China Sea by force. The navies of Vietnam, the Philippines, and Malaysia are small. So China just took what they wanted.

日本の多くの左派の人たちは、日本が軍隊を持つと、戦争になると考えます。しかし、真実は逆です。近年、南シナ海において、中国が強制的に様々な国の島を勝手に乗っ取っています。ベトナム、フィリピン、マレーシア、こうした国の海軍は小さいです。それで、中国がそのまま欲しい所を乗っ取ってしまったのです。

They also tried the same thing with Japan, in the Senkaku islands. However constant patrols by the Japanese Coast Guard, with the Japanese Maritime Self Defense Force in the background, prevented that. The Chinese saw they could not simply walk in unchallenged, so they gave up.

中国は尖閣諸島で、日本にも同じことをしました。しかし、日本の海上保安庁が常に巡視を行い、そのうしろに海上自衛隊が控えていたことで、中国の尖閣諸島への上陸を防ぎました。中国は、簡単には上陸ができなさそうだと理解したからこそ、あきらめたわけです。

I do not in any way approve of every American military action. I think their military is way too large, and they use it too much in too many countries. Yet no country, except Japan, has since 1812 attacked America.

私は、アメリカの軍事行動をすべて認めるわけではありません。

215

Chapter7 The problems of Defense after the collapse of America

アメリカ軍は大きくなりすぎたと思うし、いろいろな国で軍事力を
使いすぎだと思います。ちなみに、1812年の米英戦争以降、アメ
リカを攻撃した国は日本だけです。

Do not be deceived by enemy propaganda
敵のプロパガンダにだまされるな

There is a Japanese type of thinking, prevalent on the left, that in war
Japan was a terrible country.

日本人の、特に左派に多い考え方に、日本は戦争で恐ろしい行為
を行った、というものがあります。

That is enemy propaganda. You do not believe enemy propaganda.
Japanese people do not understand the concept of lying for your own
profit. Foreigners do it all the time.

しかしこれは、敵のプロパガンダです。敵のプロパガンダを信じて
はダメです。相手が自分の利益のために平気で嘘を言うということを、
日本人は理解していません。外国人なら、いつだってそうします。

There is something Japanese people do when dealing with foreigners.
In Japan, people are basically honest. In this country, you can make a
business deal with a handshake. I do all the time.

外国人と取引をする時にも、日本人はこのような対応をしがちで
す。日本では、人は基本的に正直です。この国では、ビジネスの取
引を握手で決めることができます。私はいつもそうします。

In America, everything must be done with a legal contract. Even
marriage contracts are common now in America.

第7章　アメリカ崩壊後の防衛問題

アメリカでは、どんな行為であっても、すべて契約書をもって行います。結婚契約書ですら、現在のアメリカでは一般的です。

But Japanese believe a person when they speak. Everything. So many foreigners have taken advantage of this. People without any qualification at all have come to Japan, advertised themselves, and gotten good jobs.

しかし日本では、人が話をすれば、その人の言うことを信じます。すべて信じます。だから数多くの外国人が、このことを利用します。男の資格、技術、知識もないのに、日本に来て、自分のことを上手く宣伝して、良い仕事を手に入れます。

In America, you would be asked to prove your qualifications, to provide references. In fact, Americans always doubt somebody they don't know. Trust is difficult in America, because there are many people who will cheat you and harm you.

アメリカでは、その人の資格を証明するための照会先を提出することが当たり前です。実際、アメリカ人は常に、知らない人を疑っています。アメリカでは、騙したり悪いことをしたりする人が数多くいるので、他人を信頼するということが難しいのです。

I myself have what I call the transmission gear in my heart. I have one personality for dealing with foreigners. And there is another one, the one I like, when I can deal with Japanese people. I am a much nicer person as a Japanese.

私は、自分の心の中に、車のトランスミッションのような、切り替え装置を持っています。そのうちの一つの人格は、外国人と取引するためのものです。もう一つの人格、私が好きな方は、日本人と取引するための人格です。私は、日本人である時の方が、はるかに優しい人間です。

Too many people on the Left just accept everything foreigners say about

217

Chapter7 The problems of Defense after the collapse of America

WWII and Japan. They have no idea most of it is to hide what terrible things foreigners did.

　左派の人は、大東亜戦争について、外国人の話を信じすぎています。このような話の本当の目的は、自分たち外国軍が行った恐ろしい行為を隠すために言っていることなのに、日本人はこうしたことを、ほとんど理解していません。

Also, Japanese people have a cultural habit of putting one's own self, family, nation in lower position compared to others. This is a very good thing in Japan, it contributes to social harmony. But when dealing with foreigners, it is disastrous.

　もう一つの日本人の文化的な特徴として、自分自身、自分の家族、自分の国を、他人や他国よりも低い位置に置こうとします。日本においては、これは良いことであり、平和な社会を作ります。でも、外国人と取引をする場合には、悲惨なことになります。

A foreigner will always lie to protect themselves, even when they are criminals. And they always exaggerate their abilities.

　自分を守るためには、たとえそれが犯罪であろうと、外国人は嘘を言います。そして、自分の能力をいつも誇張します。

When animals are in a fight, like a house cat, do you not notice that their hair stands up? This is to make them look physically bigger, more scary. Well, foreigner conversations follow the same pattern, to make the speaker look stronger, smarter, more moral.

　動物がお互いに戦う時、例えばネコがケンカをする際に、毛が立つ、という状態が分かりますか？　これは自分をもっと大きく、もっと強く見えるようにするためです。外国人の会話はこれと同じです。しゃべっている人がより強く、より頭が良く、より道徳的に見えるようにしゃべるのです。

218

第 7 章　アメリカ崩壊後の防衛問題

Japanese people just have no need for this kind of thing. As a basic thing, Japanese people are incredibly kind. But I must say, you have to be different when dealing with foreigners.

日本人には、このようなことは必要ありません。基本的に、日本人は本当に優しいです。でも、外国人とつきあう時は、違う態度が必要です。

Americans always make excessive propaganda about their enemies. Look at all the propaganda stories about President Donald Trump since people realized he was a serious candidate in 2016.

アメリカ人はいつも、敵に対して過度のプロパガンダをします。2016 年の大統領選挙で、トランプ氏が本格的な候補者であることをアメリカ人が理解してから後の、そのすべてのプロパガンダを見てください。

All kinds of things about his character and morals, yet none of it is true.

彼の性格や品行について、悪い噂をたくさん出していますが、全く本当のことではありません。

The truth about Japanese Imperial Forces in WWII was that they were rather well behaved. Yes, sometimes people were killed needlessly, sometimes crimes were committed.

大東亜戦争における帝国陸海軍の真実も、むしろ行儀が良かった方だと言えるでしょう。まあ時々は、不必要に人が殺されたり、犯罪が起きたこともありますが。

But in general their behavior was very good. Frankly, American forces were not so well behaved. This is because of a certain part of the American character that people feel they must always disobey authority.

Chapter7 The problems of Defense after the collapse of America

しかし、基本的に、日本軍の態度はとても良いものでした。正直に言うと、アメリカ兵の態度はあまり良くありませんでした。なぜかというと、これはアメリカ人の性格の特徴的なことでもあるのですが、彼らには常に、権力には従わないという気持ちがあるのです。

This failing was especially strong in service troops, and 80% of the US Army were service troops. That is why rape and crime by American troops was so common during the occupation years.

特に戦務部隊でこうした問題が多く、アメリカ軍の８割は戦務部隊でした。そのため、アメリカによる占領時代には、アメリカ兵によるレイプや他の犯罪が頻繁にありました。

I have heard about a comment in Japanese newspapers by a certain Morinaga Takuro. He seems to have said that if Japan was invaded by a foreign country, instead of fighting back, the noble thing to do would be to sit in our houses and wait for the enemy to come kill us.

私は、日本のテレビでよく見る評論家、森永卓郎氏のコメントを見たことがあります。彼はある対談で、もし日本が他国から侵略されたら、自分を守って戦うのではなく、敵が殺しに来るまで家で座って待つことが、高潔な行為なのだという意味の発言をしました。

He said that all the world would admire such people who would let themselves be slaughtered rather than use violence to fight back.

彼の話では、敵と戦うのではなく、自分たちが虐殺されることを許すような民族であれば、世界中の国々から称賛されるだろうということでした。

Now this amazed me. First of all, if such a case happened, the rest of the world would not look at Japan in admiration, but shock and disbelief.

この話には驚きました。まず、そのような事件が起きた場合、世

第7章　アメリカ崩壊後の防衛問題

界の他の国々は、日本を称賛するどころか、大きなショックと信じられないという気持ちで、称賛とは正反対に捉えるでしょう。

And did he ask his wife and children their opinion of this philosophy? I don't think they would agree.

それに彼は、自分の奥さんや子供たちにも、この考え方に同意するのかどうか、意見を聞いてみたのでしょうか？　私は、奥さんも子供も同意しないと思います。

The Emperor is central to a peaceful and prosperous Japan
天皇陛下を中心とする、豊かで平和な日本

But the important thing now is that Japan is facing an extreme emergency. American chaos means that Japan is going to lose a lot of trade and food imports. The number of unemployed will skyrocket in Japan.

しかし、大切なことは、日本にはまもなく、大変な危機の時代が来るということです。アメリカの混乱によって、日本の貿易は打撃を受け、食料輸入の多くを失います。また、失業する人が急増します。

We will all have to work together as one nation and one family. And that is what I ask of the Japanese Left, please help and cooperate. After all, we all want the same thing, a prosperous and peaceful Japan.

日本人は、一つの家族、一つの国家として、共に努力する必要があります。私は、日本の左派の皆さんにお願いがあります。どうか、一緒に手伝って、協力してください。結局のところ、私たちの目標は同じです。私たちは皆、豊かで平和な日本を望んでいるのです。

221

Chapter7 The problems of Defense after the collapse of America

When you protest some policy, use common sense. Everyone is going to have to make an effort.

また、何かの政策に対して抗議をする際には、常識的にお願いします。今は国民全員の努力が必要なのです。

Japan is a very lucky country that as a central pillar of our existence is the Imperial Household. This provides a unifying point for all Japanese people. All Japanese culture flows from the Emperor.

日本の中心に皇室の存在があることは、非常に幸運なことです。全国民にとっての中心となる柱は天皇陛下です。日本の文化はすべて、天皇陛下から流れてきています。

Even though as I write this, my passport is still American, I consider myself to be Japanese, the Emperor of Japan is my sovereign.

私は、このような文章を書きながらも、パスポートはまだアメリカです。しかし、私の心の中で、日本の天皇陛下は私の天皇陛下です。

A country needs a center. By promoting so much diversity, America is creating many groups with their main identity based on race, gender, or sexual identity. They no longer think of themselves as American.

国には中心点が必要です。しかしアメリカは、過度に多様性を推進したために、民族、性別、性的アイデンティティなど、多くのグループを作り出しました。その結果、彼らは自分たちをアメリカ人と考えていません。

Japan had the right approach in the annexation of Korea and Taiwan, to bind all into one into one people, equal under the Emperor.

日本はかつて、李氏朝鮮や台湾の併合を、正しいやり方で行いました。それは、天皇陛下のもとで平等な国民を創るということでした。

第 7 章　アメリカ崩壊後の防衛問題

That is America's major problem. A center was never fully developed. There never was really something that all Americans could deeply believe in. In the Vietnam war, a lot of the protest was against traditional culture. Part of the protest movement was spiritual, a search for something deep and meaningful. It was never found.

これはアメリカの一番大きな問題です。中心点が完全には開発されませんでした。アメリカ人には、全員が信じられるようなものがありませんでした。ベトナム戦争に対する反戦運動の抗議は、アメリカの伝統的な文化に対しての抗議でした。その反戦運動の一部は精神的なものでしたし、宗教的な存在感を説明できる意義深いもの、意味を探すことでした。しかし、それは見つけられませんでした。

The miscalculations of the Deep State
黒幕たちの誤算

Once the war was over and people began to embrace materialism more fully, which pleased the Deep State people, who were in the main concerned with making money. It meant that people would buy more consumer goods.

ベトナム戦争後、アメリカ人は唯物論を深く受け入れるようになりました。このことは、お金を儲けることを目的としているディープ・ステート、つまり社会の黒幕たちを喜ばせました。なぜならそれは、アメリカ人が、より多くの消費財を買うことを意味していたからです。

One's material possessions became the central pillar of American existence, there was nothing to believe in, nothing spiritual.

所有物がアメリカ人の存在の中心の柱になっても、精神的に信じられるものはありませんでした。

223

Chapter7 The problems of Defense after the collapse of America

But gradually almost every government service was privatized, making life more expensive, and less functional. This has continued until where the people are revolting.

しかし、徐々に、ほとんどの政府機関が民営化されていくにつれ、生活のコストはより高くなり、機能はより低下していきました。こうした状況が続いたために、現在のアメリカ人はそれに反発し、国内は革命状態になってきているのです。

And why revolt is occurring is because an existence that has no other purpose except acquiring more things cannot be maintained. American life had become a vast nothingness.

なぜ革命状態になってきているのか、それは、消費財のみを集める生活を維持することができないからです。アメリカ人の生活は、非常に空虚なものになりました。

I am not particularly upset by the existence of the Deep State. In any nation, there have always been powers behind the throne.

私は、ディープ・ステート、つまり黒幕の存在に対しても、そんなに怒りの感情はありません。どんな国でも、常に、玉座の裏に力を持った人たちがいます。

We have seen the American Deep State in the open since the summer of 2016, during the American Presidential campaign. It has not been a pretty sight.

2016年夏の大統領選挙期間中に、私たちはアメリカのディープ・ステートを、はっきりと目にすることができました。でも、それはあまり美しい光景ではありませんでした。

The Deep State consists of many entities, individuals and groups. One hint is people that call themselves Globalists. They can be thought of as

第7章　アメリカ崩壊後の防衛問題

Deep State. Their incompetence and greed amazes me.

　こうしたディープ・ステート、アメリカの黒幕は、様々な権力者やグループで構成されています。その一つのグループは、グローバリストです。彼らは、まずディープ・ステートと考えて良いでしょう。しかし私は、彼らの無能さと強欲さに、驚いています。

Americans exhibit extreme greed in every kind of business, and do not care about who they hurt. Take Health Care for an example. Instead of curing people, American heath care takes their money and ruins them. A sickness, accident, or just dealing with a hospital destroys people. They cannot live.

　アメリカ人というのは、どんなビジネスにおいても強欲で、誰が損をしようと気にしません。例として、健康保険を考えてみましょう。アメリカの健康保険システムは、人を治すのではなく、その人の財産を奪って、その人の生活を崩壊させます。1件の病気、事故、ちょっとした入院で、その人の生活を破壊します。

It is the same in many other areas, over several decades the American system has evolved to extract the maximum amount of wealth possible from the American people.

　他の多くの分野でも、アメリカ社会のシステムは同じです。長年にわたってアメリカ社会は、アメリカ国民から最大限の財産を引き出すように進化してきたのです。

And then the Deep State, establishment people are surprised when the American people turned to a complete outsider, Donald Trump, and elected him President.

　そして国民は、完璧なアウトサイダー、ドナルド・トランプ氏を大統領に選びました。このことに、ディープ・ステート、黒幕たちは驚いているのです。

225

Chapter7 The problems of Defense after the collapse of America

No he can't fix things, the troubles are too deep in American society. But as I write this, the American Right still has hope.

しかし、繰り返しになりますが、トランプ氏にもアメリカを立て直すことはできません。アメリカという国の抱えている問題が深すぎます。それでも、私はこの文章を書きながら、右派にはまだ望みがあると思っています。

And the Deep State is totally disorganized. There is no coordination between the various groups and individuals, everyone simply works for their own profit. Because of the American Gun Industry, private Americans are well armed. I have read of efforts by American gun companies to sell automatic weapons to 8 year olds in Iowa. The companies make them in bright plastic colors to make them attractive to children.

ディープ・ステート、黒幕たちは、とても無秩序です。様々なグループと個人の間に共同作業はありません。皆が自分の利益のためだけに動いているのです。アメリカの銃の業界のおかげで、アメリカ人は実に多くの武器を持っています。私は、アイオワ州の８歳の子供に自動小銃を売るために、銃器製造会社がいかに努力をしているかという記事を読みました。この会社は、自動小銃を子供たちにとって魅力的なものにするために、銃のプラスチック部品を明るい色で作っているというのです。

So by this, the private population is very well armed.

こうした努力によって、アメリカ国民は武器をたくさん所持するようになったわけです。

Because of so many useless wars, particularly in the Middle East, there are many combat experienced Americans.

また、数多くの無益な戦争をしたおかげで、アメリカには、特に

第7章　アメリカ崩壊後の防衛問題

中近東での戦争経験がある元アメリカ兵がたくさんいます。

And since the military is a volunteer military, they are basically Right wing. They have organized themselves into private militias, and they voted for Donald Trump for President.

現在の米軍は志願制度の軍隊ですから、基本的に兵士は政治的には右派です。こうした元兵士が民兵組織を作って、ドナルド・トランプ氏を大統領にするために投票したのです。

They are 100,000 strong. They have the ability to conduct a successful revolution. And they are aware to the social and political realities of America.

民兵組織には10万人ものメンバーがいます。彼らには実際に革命を成功させる能力があります。それと、彼らはアメリカの社会的、政治的な現実を理解しています。

In their extreme greed, the Deep State has brought America to a revolutionary situation. This is highly irresponsible to the American people, and the world. And in the armed militia movement, they have created a force that can destroy them. This is not intelligent thinking on the part of the elites.

自分たちの強欲さで、ディープ・ステート、黒幕たちは、アメリカに革命状態を作り出しました。これは、アメリカ人と世界中の人々に対して、非常に無責任なことです。しかも、それによって民兵組織、つまり自分たちを消し去る可能性を持った集団を作り出してしまったのです。これは、エリートの考えた聡明な政策などではありません。

227

Chapter8 The Great Escape

Chapter 8
The Great Escape
大脱走

The extravagant escape plans of the Rich
富裕層の華麗なる逃亡計画

And having created this disaster, what plan do the people of the Deep State have?

それで、このような大失態を演じたディープ・ステートの人たちは、今後どうしていくのでしょうか？

Escape. They are planning to run away. There is a new fad in America, the people who follow it are called Preppers. It comes from the word preparation. It means people who stockpile food and guns in preparation for natural disaster or social collapse.

逃亡です。彼らは逃げ出すつもりです。今、アメリカには新しい流行があり、その人たちは「プレッパーズ（Preppers）」と呼ばれています。「準備する」という意味の英語 "preparation" という単語から来ています。この言葉の意味するところは、自然災害や社会の崩壊に備えて、銃と食料を備蓄する、ということです。

One source says that over 50% of Silicon valley billionaires have some kind of escape plan.

ある記事では、シリコンバレーの億万長者のうち半分が、何かしらの逃亡計画を持っていると書かれていました。

第8章　大脱走

What are these plans like? At the low end, they involve buying guns and storing non perishable food in the house. The next step up involves buying a vacation home in a remote rural area. The plan is to escape there when riots start.

彼らの逃亡計画は、このようなものです。まず手始めに銃と保存のきく食料を買って、家に蓄えます。その次に、遠い田舎に家を買います。そして、暴動が始まったら、そこへ逃げるという計画です。

A step up from this is a company called Survival Condo Project in the state of Kansas. They have taken a former Atlas nuclear missile silo, and rebuilt it into luxury apartments. A full floor apartment sells for 3 million dollars, half floor dwellings are half price.

さらに上を目指すなら、カンザス州にある「サバイバル・コンド・プロジェクト」がオススメです。これは、かつての核兵器、アトラス・ミサイルの地下格納庫を豪華なアパートに作り直したものです。ワンフロアのアパートは 300 万ドル（約 3 億円）で販売され、その半分の広さなら値段は半額です。

At this location in Concordia Kansas, all 12 apartments have been sold. The complex is guarded by armed guards. The company is building other locations. Other companies are taking the same pattern and rebuilding natural caverns and underground government installations for the rich.

このカンザス州コンコーディア市の場合、12 あるアパートは全て売り切れています。施設は武装した警備員に守られており、この会社は、別の場所でも同じような施設を建設中です。また、他の会社は、こうしたお金持ちの人々のために、鍾乳洞や、地下にある政府施設をリフォーム中です。

And there is New Zealand. For the very rich, that is regarded as a comfortable country in which to spend the Apocalypse. The number of

Chapter8 The Great Escape

rich Americans buying real estate there has greatly increased in recent years.

さらに、ニュージーランドもあります。ここは、超お金持ちの人たちが、世の終末を過ごすのに、とても快適な国です。ここ数年、ニュージーランドに不動産を購入する裕福なアメリカ人の数が、急激に増えているそうです。

It seems that Bill Gates himself has chosen Japan. He has bought a large piece of land in Karuizawa, and is remodeling it to his own taste.

ちなみにビル・ゲイツ氏は、日本を選んだようです。彼は軽井沢に広大な土地を購入し、自分の好みに作り直しています。

Japanese people should learn from history
日本人は、今こそ歴史に学ぶべき

I cannot over emphasize how irresponsible this is. Create a revolutionary situation in America by greedy business practices, and then run overseas.

こうした行為がどれほど無責任なことなのかを、ここでは力説しません。彼らは強欲な商売によってアメリカ国内に革命的な状態を作り出し、その後、海外へ逃げ去るのです。

That is the reason for this quote at the beginning of this book:

それが、この本の冒頭にある引用の理由です。

"Merchants have no country. The mere spot they stand on does not constitute so strong an attachment as that from which they draw their gains." —— Thomas Jefferson

第8章　大脱走

商人に国境はない。彼らにとっては、国よりも利益が大切なのだ。
——トーマス・ジェファーソン（第3代アメリカ合衆国大統領）

For the future of the planet, we should work to create a form of government where the greed of a few individuals cannot destroy it. I think the Tokugawa government of feudal Japan deserves a lot more study.

地球の将来のために、ひと握りの強欲な人たちによって潰されることのない政府の形を作る必要があります。そのためには、私は、日本の徳川幕府をもっと深く勉強するべきだと思います。

In that age, the people with the power to rule did not control the money. The people with the money could not have the power to rule. In any case, for the future, we need to create leaders with a sense of mission and obligation, for the betterment of mankind.

江戸時代、人々を支配している権力者は、お金をコントロールすることができませんでした。また、単にお金を持っている人が権力者になるということも不可能でした。とにかく、将来のために、人類のために、使命感と義務感を持ったリーダーを育てる必要があります

With the collapse of America, the world is in for a very difficult time. Particularly Japan, our ties with America are many and deep. But I have faith in the ability of the Japanese people. In 15, maybe even 10 years, Japan will be the most admirable country in the world, with the highest standard of living, the happiest people. That is what I strive for.

アメリカの崩壊によって、世界はより困難な時代に入ります。特に日本は、アメリカとの縁が深く、接点が数多くあります。しかし私は、日本人の能力を信じています。15年後、あるいは10年後に、日本は世界で最も魅力的な国となり、最も豊かな生活と、最も幸せな国民の国となるでしょう。私も、その将来のために努力していきたいと思います。

231

Afterward
おわりに

It is difficult to keep up with events in the United States. Just as I finished this book, I find news of Left wing activists burning churches in rural America. They wish to provoke a violent Right wing reaction.

アメリカ合衆国の国内情勢の変化に、遅れずについて行くことは非常に難しいです。ちょうどこの本を書き終えたころにも、左派がアメリカの地方にある教会に放火しているニュースを見つけました。左派によるこうした事件は、右派の暴力的な反動を誘発することが目的です。

No political force is capable of peaceful solution. Americans have not experienced war domestically since 1865, they let their passions go out of control. This is particularly true of the Left.

もう、平和的な解決が出来る政治組織はありません。アメリカ人は国内では 1865 年以来、戦争の経験がありませんし、彼らの感情は制御不能です。これは、特に左派において当てはまる真実です。

At present as I write this, the violence is basically physical assault, again primarily conducted by the Left, at political rallies and meetings. But it can only be a matter of time before guns become involved, then many will die.

私が本書で書いてきたように、こうした暴力は基本的に、政治大会や政治的な集会で身体的な暴行として行われており、そのほとんどが左派によって行われたものです。しかし、こうした場で銃が使用されるようになるのは時間の問題であり、その時には、数多くの

おわりに

人が死ぬでしょう。

How many people are in the Antifa? Searching the net, I found two hard figures. Antifa has 18,000 twitter followers in New York City, and 6,000 in Philadelphia.

反ファシズム運動には何人のメンバーがいるのでしょうか？　ネットで探してみたところ、2つの数字を見つけました。反ファシズム運動のツイッターには、ニューヨーク市で 18,000 人、フィラデルフィア市で 6,000 人のフォロワーがいます。

Extrapolating this to the country at large, we can estimate up to 100,000 followers. In guerrilla warfare, you need at least 10 times the amount of troops to guerrillas to win.

これを全国で推計すると、約 10 万人のフォロワーがいると考えられます。ゲリラ戦で勝つためには、ゲリラの数に対して 10 倍の兵士が必要だと言われています。

America would need about 1 million infantry soldiers, this would be a serious strain on the active duty forces, Reserve forces would need to be mobilized.

つまり、アメリカには 100 万の歩兵が必要ということになります。しかし、現役の部隊ではこれだけの調達は厳しく、予備役を動員しなければなりません。

It is a serious threat. The FBI has learned that last summer, during the G20 summit in Germany, American Antifa members from Oakland California traveled to Hamburg Germany and participated in the violence. While there, they met with representatives of AQAP (Al Qaeda in the Arabian Peninsula). These people are helping American Antifa get access to bomb and chemical weapons. One American traveled to Syria to meet further with them.

233

Afterward

　これはまさに本格的な脅威です。FBI によれば、2017 年の夏に
ドイツで開催された G20 サミットの際に、カリフォルニア州オーク
ランド市の反ファシズム運動のメンバーが、ドイツのハンブルク
市まで行って暴動に参加したということです。しかも彼らはその時
に、AQAP（アラビア半島のアルカーイダ）の代表と会っているの
です。この AQAP という組織は、アメリカの反ファシズム運動に
対して、爆弾と化学兵器を得られるよう、手助けをしています。さ
らに、この AQAP とより深い会談をするために、1 人のアメリカ
人がシリアへ渡ったということです。

In the end, I think the Right will prevail. In the militia movement,
they have a disciplined and capable military force. The standing
military forces are basically Right wing politically.

　とはいえ、やはり最後には、右派がこの内乱に勝つでしょう。民
兵組織による運動には規律があり、機能的で訓練された部隊があり
ます。しかも、現役の連邦政府軍は、基本的に政治的には右派です。

The Antifa, the primary violent force of the Left, is childish and
undisciplined. But they will continue to provoke events until they
are smashed.

　左派の基本部隊である反ファシズム運動は、子供っぽく、規律が
ありません。しかし彼らも、潰されるまでは暴動を誘発し続けるで
しょう。

President Trump is not powerful enough to bring peace to
America by himself. The Left hates him viscerally. The Republican
party, loyal to corporate sponsors, refuses to cooperate with him.

　トランプ大統領は、自分自身でアメリカに平和をもたらす力はあ
りません。左派は、不合理で感情的なやり方で、彼に嫌悪感、つま
りヘイトの感情を持っています。彼の所属する共和党は、企業のス

おわりに

ポンサーに忠実であり、トランプ大統領に協力することを拒否しています。

The only real likely winner in this mess is the Christian Fundamentalist movement, I think that they will be the dominant political force in future America.

こうした混乱の中で勝つ組織はキリスト教原理主義のみであり、彼らが将来のアメリカで支配的な政治勢力となるでしょう。

But since they are a religious movement, the conflict will then evolve into religious Civil War. These are among the most terrible kinds of war you can imagine.

しかし、あくまで彼らは宗教のための運動です。なので、いずれアメリカの混乱は、宗教的な内乱へと発展するでしょう。そして、この戦争は、私たちが想像することが出来る中で、最も恐ろしい戦争なのです。

マックス・フォン・シュラー

Sources
情報源

Since this is an ongoing event, much of my material comes from Right wing web sites. I always check the things they say on google, and other sites.

こうした現在進行形の動きについて、私は、ほとんどの情報を右派的なサイトから手に入れています。そして、そのサイトで書かれていることを、いつも別の所で二重に確認しています。

The problem is that most main stream media is absolutely skewed towards the Left. In some cases I have caught them in lies, for example concerning the number of marchers at a November 4 rally in New York City.

問題は、従来のマスメディアが、完全に左派寄りになっていることです。私は、いくつかのケースで彼らの嘘を見つけました。例えば、2017年11月4日の、ニューヨーク市におけるデモ行進者の数についてです。

Newsweek reported only about 300 supporters for the Antifa marching on November 4th. But checking on google, I found a video showing 20 minutes of marchers, 6 or so columns across.

ニューズウィーク誌は、反ファシズム運動の支持者は300人ぐらいしかいなかったと報道しました。しかし、グーグルで確認すると、参加者が6列くらいに並んだデモ行進が、20分も続いている動画を見つけました。

That would be at least 10,000 or more. Why does the media downplay the event? I don't know.

情報源

　これは、少なくとも 1 万人以上になるはずです。なぜマスメディアは、こうした事件を控えめに伝えたがるのでしょうか？　私には分かりません。

Some sites to check:

　以下は、面白い情報があるサイトです。ぜひ、チェックしてみてください。

Infowars　https://www.infowars.com/

Here I found information about Drag Queens teaching primary school students in public libraries in New York City and San Francisco.　But this site exaggerates many many things, such the Las Vegas shooting of October 1st 2017.　You have to double check things they say on google.

　私はこのサイトで、女装した男性の同性愛者が、ニューヨーク市とサンフランシスコ市の市立図書館で小学生たちに教えているという情報を見つけました。しかし、このサイトは、数多くのことを大げさに誇張しています。例えば、2017 年 10 月 1 日に起こったラスベガスでの銃乱射事件などです。なので、どんなことでも、グーグル等で二重に確認する必要があります。

Breitbart　http://www.breitbart.com/

This site is more reliable than Infowars, but still check them on google.

　このサイトは、上記の Infowars よりは信頼性がありますが、やはりグーグル等で確認した方が良いでしょう。

Sources

Zero Hedge   http://www.zerohedge.com/

Unz Review   https://www.unz.com/

These two sites provide good articles and information on the conflict in America.

この二つのサイトには、アメリカ国内の混乱についての良い情報があります。

Itsgoingdown.org   https://itsgoingdown.org/

This is the site for Antifa.

これは、反ファシズム運動のサイトです。

Refusefascism.org   https://refusefascism.org/

This site is Antifa, and concerned with ongoing demonstrations against the Trump administration. A recent check showed coverage of Demonstrations on November 4th and 18th 2017.

このサイトも、反ファシズム運動のものです。特に、進行中の反トランプ政権のデモについて書かれています。最近では、2017年11月4日と18日のデモについて書かれていました。

◆著者◆
マックス・フォン・シュラー (Max von Schuler)

本名、マックス・フォン・シュラー小林。

元海兵隊・歴史研究家。ドイツ系アメリカ人。

1974年岩国基地に米軍海兵隊として来日、その後日本、韓国で活動。

退役後、国際基督教大学、警備会社を経て、役者として「釣りバカ日誌8」等、ナレーターとして「足立美術館音声ガイド」等、日本で活動。

現在は結婚式牧師、「日出処から」代表講師。

著書に『アメリカ人が語る アメリカが隠しておきたい日本の歴史』(ハート出版)『太平洋戦争 アメリカに嵌められた日本』(ワック)『アメリカ白人の闇』(桜の花出版) などがある。

アメリカ人が語る **日本人に隠しておけないアメリカの"崩壊"**

平成 29 年 12 月 24 日　第 1 刷発行

著　者　マックス・フォン・シュラー
発行者　日高裕明
発　行　株式会社ハート出版

〒 171-0014 東京都豊島区池袋 3-9-23
TEL.03(3590)6077　FAX.03(3590)6078
ハート出版ホームページ　http://www.810.co.jp

©Max von Schuler Printed in Japan 2017
定価はカバーに表示してあります。
ISBN978-4-8024-0041-1　C0031
乱丁・落丁本はお取り替えいたします。ただし古書店で購入したものはお取り替えできません。

印刷・中央精版印刷株式会社

アメリカ人が語る
アメリカが隠しておきたい日本の歴史

「真実を語ること、それはヘイトスピーチではありません」――。海兵隊出身の著者が、母国アメリカの"嘘"を告発。本当の歴史を、日米2カ国語で併記。

マックス・フォン・シュラー 著
ISBN978-4-8024-0028-2　本体 1500 円

最強兵器としての地政学
あなたも国際政治を予測できる！

トランプ大統領の誕生を、唯一、正確に予測した書。2色刷で分かりやすい、地政学入門の決定版！

藤井厳喜 著
ISBN978-4-8024-0023-7　本体 1500 円

戦争犯罪国はアメリカだった！
英国人ジャーナリストが明かす東京裁判70年の虚妄

「真のA級戦犯」は東條英機らでなく、対日戦争を仕掛けたルーズベルト、チャーチル、スターリンである。

ヘンリー・S・ストークス 著　藤田裕行 訳
ISBN978-4-8024-0016-9　本体 1600 円

ルーズベルトは米国民を裏切り日本を戦争に引きずり込んだ
アメリカ共和党元党首H・フィッシュが暴く日米戦の真相

稀代の政治家が、隠蔽された開戦当時の状況を証言。

青柳武彦 著
ISBN978-4-8024-0034-3　本体 1600 円